you don't have to be eve

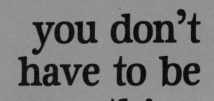

you don't have to be everything

Poems for Girls Becoming Themselves

edited by

DIANA WHITNEY

· ·

illustrations by Cristina González,
Kate Mockford, Stephanie Singleton

Workman Publishing
New York

Library of Congress Cataloging-in-Publication Data is available.

ISBN: 978-1-5235-1099-3

Design by Rae Ann Spitzenberger

Cover illustration by Kate Mockford

Cristina González: Inside cover, v, vi–vii, viii–ix, x, 3, 4, 36, 38, 41, 45, 48, 51, 92, 95, 96, 99, 100, 101, 102, 103, 104, 105, 109, 136, 166

Kate Mockford: ii, 22, 25, 27, 29, 33, 35, 72, 75, 76–77, 78, 81, 82, 83, 84, 85, 87, 91, 124, 126, 129, 130, 132–133, 135, 164

Stephanie Singleton: Back cover/flaps, 6, 8, 9, 11, 12, 17, 19, 20, 21, 52, 54, 57, 58, 60, 61, 63, 64, 65, 66, 69, 70–71, 110, 112, 115, 116, 119, 121, 122, 155, 156

Workman books are available at special discounts when purchased in bulk for premiums and sales promotions as well as for fund-raising or educational use. Special editions or book excerpts can also be created to specification. For details, contact the Special Sales Director at specialmarkets@workman.com.

Workman Publishing Co., Inc.
225 Varick Street
New York, NY 10014-4381
workman.com

WORKMAN is a registered trademark of Workman Publishing Co., Inc.

Printed in China
First printing February 2021

10 9 8 7 6 5 4 3 2 1

FOR
AVA AND
CARMEN

contents

5 / LONGING

6 / SHAME

7 / SADNESS

8 / BELONGING

INTRODUCTION

The summer I was thirteen, I locked myself in my room and kept the shades drawn. I wanted that darkness to mirror how I felt inside: lonely, unlovable, ashamed. I listened to my favorite songs over and over, imagining the lyrics were written to my private heart. In my isolation, I didn't believe anyone could understand how I felt.

I was carrying a secret like a swallowed stone. For many years, I would share that weight only with a therapist. Even my closest friends didn't know I'd been in a twisted relationship with another girl, that we'd been physically intimate, that we'd cut ourselves to try to prove our love, that my parents had found out and forbidden me to see her.

I remember spending a rainy afternoon that August writing a poem in a cabin in Maine's North Woods. Showers battered the roof, and the pine trees bowed over in submission. The world was gray green, clouds pressing at the windows. Outside my door, my little brothers and sister were playing board games, laughing and eating Triscuits.

My longing was immense—bigger than that cabin, bigger than the forest. I channeled it into a poem— an ode to the Beatles, woven from their song titles, written from a girl who was "born into the magic 20 years too late." It was not a brilliant poem, but that didn't matter. I'd discovered the thrill of composition, an emotional release. That creative energy lifted me out of myself, and I ventured into the kitchen to read it to my mother. Mercifully, she didn't laugh. She told me she loved it.

●●●

When I envisioned a poetry anthology for girls and young people, I wanted to collect the voices I wish I'd heard when I was a teen. Strong voices, lonely voices, angry, elated, or curious ones. Voices from the LGBTQ+ community, turning their experiences into song. I wanted to affirm many kinds of "girlhood," find writers who challenge cultural norms and resist the stifling expectations of gender.

I love poetry because it opens a window into the interior world. Poems may rage, lament, celebrate, or question, but they remain rooted in emotional truth, offering what W. H. Auden calls "a clear statement of mixed feelings." Unlike self-help or how-to books,

I wanted
to collect
the voices
I wish
I'd heard
when I was
a teen.

You're strong and complicated and worthy of love.

poetry does not try to fix anything. Its language is heightened, compressed, charged with power. It allows moments of intensity and moments of quiet reflection. It can mirror our shifting, intricate selves.

I've organized this book by emotional experience so you can flip through and find poems for different moods. But let these chapter headings be suggestions, not prescriptions. One person's angry poem may evoke sadness in another. A poem about a joyful occasion may spark yearning or loneliness in some readers. No reaction is the wrong one.

Poetry offers a space for vulnerability. I hope this book gives you permission to be vulnerable too.

●●●

"You do not have to be good," writes Mary Oliver in her poem "Wild Geese." My younger daughter, Carmen, looked startled when I read her this line. Her eyes lit up. "Does that mean I can be bad?" she asked, amazed after years of messages from the world about improving her behavior, attitude, schoolwork, clothes, looks, body, self.

"Maybe," I said. "Or maybe it's that you're more than just good or bad. You're strong and complicated and worthy of love. You don't need to apologize for yourself. You don't have to be everything."

I keep returning to this promise: *You do not have to be good.* Oliver's poem calls to our imagination and reassures us that we are already enough. We are resilient humans, connected to all creation. We aren't broken or shameful or in need of fixing.

As you read these diverse writers and share their experiences, I hope you can embrace your own contradictions. I hope these poems offer some freedom from the restrictive oppositions of *good/bad, smart/stupid, hot/ugly, sluts/prudes, cool kids/losers* that the world imposes on us—in school, at home, online, and in the media.

May this book help you release the illusion of your own inadequacy. May the poems let you live into the complexity and fullness of who you are—and who you are becoming.

1 seeking

When I was fifteen, a friend's mother once commented that we teenagers were "in discovery mode." I liked the way this sounded, although I wasn't sure what she meant. Now I see that we were seeking—looking for meaning in ourselves and in the world. Seeking is a state of questioning, never an easy existence. It contains doubt and discomfort, anxiety and confusion, insecurity and indecision. And it doesn't magically end in adulthood.

But seeking also offers a brave open-endedness, the practice of becoming "comfortable with uncertainty," as Buddhist teacher Pema Chödrön counsels. The poets here would agree. They are explorers, whether they're seeking love and connection, like Sahar Romani in her coming-out poem, or trying to grasp a native language, like Marci Calabretta Cancio-Bello in "Origin/Adoption."

Margaret Atwood recounts a dream of flying—a seeking beyond the human realm—then wakes into a painfully earthbound body. Trans writer Stephanie Burt seeks self-definition and a renewed experience of girlhood. Meanwhile, Elizabeth Spires asks a series of unanswerable "Questions for Google." Her spare questions are for all seekers, of all ages, genders and cultures, on a journey toward understanding.

FINAL EXAM STEPHANIE

Stephanie Burt

Please turn in or leave behind any scratch materials. You
have now agreed to follow all the rules. Good girls will be
notified sooner. Next year you are going. You have to look
forward to until.

Like walking out of an uncompleted pencil sketch, an
unprimed canvas, the torn-off end of a page, like being
a bracket in the fragment of ancient Greek that I
encountered in my best friend's photograph. Nobody

is going to report me if I break down, break up, break in
three, like a bone left to us from beach week's campfire
feast

> like the page after the last
> page of a comic book
>
> like whatever takes place under the oblong
> gleam on microscope glass
>
> like the white space between the grays
> of a birch branch shadow on snow
>
> like the aluminum ladder in our basement
> on its side on the cold concrete going nowhere

It's June. I have a new and golden pendant, a folding hand
mirror, a calculator too. Its heft in my hand grins like
a mirror pointed back at the sun.

What is this air, this space in which nobody rewards

me for conformity,

or punishes me, or keeps

track of my time, what I wear, how I see

myself, or tries to tell me what my name should be?

ORIGIN/ADOPTION

Marci Calabretta Cancio-Bello

My first mother placed inside my mouth
a thick tongue / a curled tongue
prone to quick rolling music
and bramble-berried consonants
I would never speak to her.
These days, on this other hemisphere
I twist my second mother's words
from my tongue as I do
the fruit from my neighbor's tree:
geu-rhim / cham-eh / / fig and yellow
melon arching over the sidewalk,
ripening into dark hills / deep sun.
These days, I peel this craving
already budded with discomfort,
recover utterances too long untouched,
as if I could know the correct
taste of each vowel / inflections
sweet on my fingers and chin.

FLYING INSIDE YOUR OWN BODY

Margaret Atwood

Your lungs fill & spread themselves,
wings of pink blood, and your bones
empty themselves and become hollow.
When you breathe in you'll lift like a balloon
and your heart is light too & huge,
beating with pure joy, pure helium.
The sun's white winds blow through you,
there's nothing above you,
you see the earth now as an oval jewel,
radiant & seablue with love.
It's only in dreams you can do this.
Waking, your heart is a shaken fist,
a fine dust clogs the air you breathe in;
the sun's a hot copper weight pressing straight
down on the thick pink rind of your skull.
It's always the moment just before gunshot.
You try & try to rise but you cannot.

QUESTIONS FOR GOOGLE

Elizabeth Spires

What does it mean and why does it matter?
How do I get from here to there?
Where is the line that cannot be crossed?
Why is the first time the best?

Who will be coming and when will they get here?
How long will it last before it is over?
Who has the right and why do they have it?
Who is the most important one?

What did it mean and why did it matter?
If all is lost, how will I find it?
If not now, then when?
Are you *real*? Do you even exist?

THE YEAR I TELL MY PARENTS I AM A HOMOSEXUAL

Sahar Romani

Words animal
out of our mouths
splinter
through the kitchen window
across the front yard
beyond the red wind chimes
above the pines
everyone can hear us
the woman pulling weeds next door
Korean kids riding bicycles up
and down the cul-de-sac
even the crows
hunched on traffic lights a mile south
arguments asymmetrical
muscular in breath
no one ready for surrender
we take refuge in bedrooms
and versions of God
we love each other so much
so much we love we other
tomorrow morning
we'll say salam
peace be with you
wailaikum salam
and with you
peace

BIKE RIDE WITH OLDER BOYS
Laura Kasischke

The one I didn't go on.

I was thirteen,
and they were older.
I'd met them at the public pool. I must

have given them my number. I'm sure

I'd given them my number,
knowing the girl I was . . .

It was summer. My afternoons
were made of time and vinyl.
My mother worked,
but I had a bike. They wanted

to go for a ride.
Just me and them. I said
okay fine, I'd
meet them at the Stop-n-Go
at four o'clock.
And then I didn't show.

I have been given a little gift—
something sweet
and inexpensive, something
I never worked or asked or said
thank you for, most
days not aware
of what I have been given, or what I missed—

because it's that, too, isn't it?
I never saw those boys again.
I'm not as dumb
as they think I am

but neither am I wise. Perhaps

it is the best
afternoon of my life. Two
cute and older boys
pedaling beside me—respectful, awed. When we

turn down my street, the other girls see me . . .

Everything as I imagined it would be.

Or, I am in a vacant field. When I
stand up again, there are bits of glass and gravel
ground into my knees.
I will never love myself again.
Who knew then
that someday I would be

thirty-seven, wiping
crumbs off the kitchen table with a sponge, remembering
them, thinking
of this—

those boys still waiting
outside the Stop-n-Go, smoking
cigarettes, growing older.

AWAY FROM HOME
Paige Buffington

Children run in Nike Airs, in Converse or barefoot, break dirt
backbones of dry washes, skeletons of cattle. This is where you are—

where you asked Cheii for the name of sudden spring storms, what happened to the twins left alone
in the car. They're buried near the yellow brush—you can see where the earth was broken
from where you are.

The trailer in Pinedale is sun-faded, abandoned now. You slept beside dogs beneath a truck
camper, nobody checked or asked where you are. Do they still ask? Where you are;

black horses run until they're mistaken for monsoons, manes tangle in electricity lines.
Children tiptoe to touch coal hooves. Death spins like ornaments along highways where you are—

Snow backbones the New Mexico/Arizona stateline. Young men shoot wild horses, two hundred
dollars a head. *The babies need food and diapers.* Truck beds filled with broken bodies where
you are—

You still see Cheii watch deer shake first snow from their ears, still hear his sisters say, *I wish he didn't eat sweets, potatoes so much. You know, he always asked where you are.*

For years, you've walked counter-clockwise through homes, struggled to remember what to say when you brush your hair at night. You've looked for the hanging chains of basketball hoops close to where you are.

You once shook the hand of the man who named the holy skin behind the ear. Is this the word for planet or that sacred, soft skin? Paige, you can't remember from where you are.

ON CRESCENTS & TRANSITION & WANING

Kayleb Rae Candrilli

In the moments just before
anesthesia took me

to the bottom of the ocean (and then back),
I looked down my hospital gown

and admired, for the last time,
the fullness of this original body.

My original body had many marvels
but I always wished it

for someone else—spent
years daydreaming of my flesh

neatly disassembled, and sent
to more deserving homes.

But you cannot give yourself
away quite like this.

A scalpel and my breast tissue
became biological

waste. My body shrunk
to its new original. And it feels

important to say, that now,
under all this almost newness,

I can watch my own heart as it beats.
I can look at my life more

closely than ever, and how beautiful
it is, really, just under the skin,

alive & alive & alive—
like a warm moon.

LOST & FOUND

Amy Dryansky

I lost the color red: wagon, stop sign, corduroy jumper.
I lost the park when it began to thunder
and we waited out the storm
in a bunker of wet, gray wool, rubber toes
touching to protect us from lightning.
I lost the sisters who babysat when my mother
allowed herself to get desperate,
the girl on the fourth floor
who dropped her cat off the fire escape
six times before it broke a leg.
I lost the buckeye trees, two long blocks
to school, the intersection I learned to cross,
the man in the car with something on his lap
he wanted me to see. I saw.
I lost the Band-Aid colored slip
peeking out from my teacher's dress
as she read to us from Grimm's, the book fanned out
to where the thoughtless, innocent, hungry
wrens erase Hansel's breadcrumb trail.
I lost the name of the boy with dark eyes
we drove home from school, the two of us in back
elbowing, smiling. Sometimes I think
I'm still looking for him.
I lost the room I shared with my sister, narrow bed
where I looked out at the sky,
and I lost my sister. She's back, but not really.
I lost the first day of 6th grade, stepping off the bus
in my platform shoes, Meg asking me

if her paisley shirt was see-through.
I said no. That's what friends do.
I lost Soul Train, the Bump, *Superstitious*,
doing nothing, taking turns, doing nothing.
I lost my boyfriend teaching me
to kiss: *put your tongue here.*
I lost books I stole from my parents: Sartre, Camus,
Beckett, Eliot, *In Watermelon Sugar*, and thought,
"Well, what is this? What am I
supposed to know?" I lost paintings I accepted
without hesitation: nudity, violence, abstraction and the artist
who said I looked like a Picasso
etching, the kind where the women are gourd-shaped,
naked, missing one eye and I wondered
how he could see that. Did he
see that? I lost a through-line, bellwether,
gravitational pull, the point
where rays eventually intersect. I failed geometry
twice. Followed no marked path. Held on
to my radar or whatever it is
signaling OK, OK, you-my-sweet-girl-are-done.

2 loneliness

Loneliness is an all-too-familiar part of growing up. If you miss someone, if you have no one to confide in, if you've been judged or misunderstood or bullied, the ache can be excruciating. Wendy Guerra captures the feeling of being excluded in her poem "Playing Hide and Seek." Talin Tahajian describes a sense of alienation, the strangeness of being talked at by people who "want more" of her. Sometimes feeling lonely when you're with others is worse than being alone.

But solitude can offer insight and introspection. Lying awake in bed before the first day of school, Elizabeth Acevedo's fifteen-year-old speaker, Xiomara (otherwise known as *The Poet X*), feels acutely all the ways she is changing and "beginning." Melody Lee reflects on her solitary childhood spent playing outside, not caring that she was different from the other girls: "I got muddy, dirty and beautiful."

There's an intimacy with the self that grows slowly under conditions of long quiet and aloneness. Trying to find self-acceptance takes patience and time. In her poem "self-portraiture," Fariha Róisín realizes she must be gentle with herself on the journey: "the process is about letting yourself in."

PLAYING HIDE AND SEEK
Wendy Guerra

With my face buried in my arm   without cheating   with my back facing out
leaning against a tree   I counted to infinity while they hid
one one thousand   two one thousand   and when I opened my eyes   nighttime
Where is everyone?   So much time spent looking for them
One   two   three   four   five   six   seven   eight   nine   ten
How far away   how alone   how lost in the courtyard of my own game.

QUESTIONS ASKED TO ME WHEN I WAS TEN

S. Erin Batiste

What are you? Why are you here? What neighborhood do you live in? So you go to the good school? Do you think you're smart? Is your family rich? Where are you from? Is your hair real? Can I touch it? What are you mixed with? Well why do you have a French last name? How do you say your last name? Do you speak French? Why do you have an accent? Where is your accent from? Why do you wear dresses everyday? What are you reading? Do you think you're special? Where do you really live? What does your father do? Are your parents married? Why did your father marry her? Does he love her? Why is she so dark? Do you and your little sister have the same father? Why is she darker than you? Why are you so skinny? Why are you dressed like that? Where did you come from? Is your father white? Is your father Spanish? Is your father Hispanic? Is your father mixed? Wait, what is he? Why are his eyes green? Are you just plain black? But you have European features. But you're pretty. Why are you always reading? Why did your family move here? What are you? Is that all your hair? Why do you have freckles? Do you ever wear pants? Where were you born? Where are you really from? Where are your parents from? Where are your grandparents from? What about their parents' parents? How do you get your hair like that? Why do you look so different? Why are your eyes shaped that way? Are you sure you're not half-Korean? Chinese? Japanese? Vietnamese? Indian? Native? Mexican? Cuban?

Brazilian? Guatemalan? Salvadoran? Who in your family is white? Just black black huh? What's in those books? What's wrong with you? Why do you look like that? Is your hair a weave? What are you? What are you doing here? Who do you think you are? Why are you angry? Why are you getting so upset? Why are you crying, I'm just asking questions.

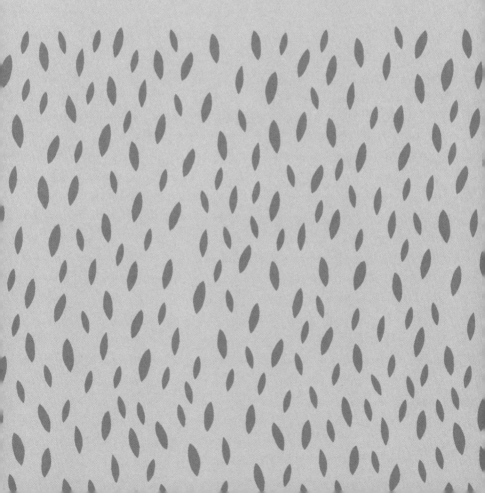

SOLITUDE

Franny Choi

I hope no one comes to my party, I said out loud,
and meant it. In the email, I tried to sound too busy to care

like, *I'm having too much sex to waste time
on proper punctuation*, pretending it's not
                            the other way around.

Laura convinced me to jump
in the Narragansett Bay on my birthday—
February. There's no good word
for the opposite of fire,
the ice's sear & split, how it beckons the blood
        toward what means to end it.

                        Oh god, I gasped over and over
as we stumbled through the snow back to the car,
me and my burning legs.

Now that's my kind of intimacy—

                                    faceless, salty,
no wondering how my jokes are going over,

just running straight toward warmth
as my skin bursts open in shock.

NIGHT BEFORE FIRST DAY OF SCHOOL

Elizabeth Acevedo

As I lie in bed,
thinking of this new school year,

I feel myself
stretching my skin apart.

Even with my Amazon frame,
I feel too small for all that's inside me.

I want to break myself open
like an egg smacked hard against an edge.

Teachers always say
that each school year is a new start:

but even before this day
I think I've been beginning.

GROWING UP

Melody Lee

They played inside with dollhouses
and toy kitchens.
I played outside, in the woods,
climbing trees, building forts.
They liked Barbie dolls. I did, too,
but I especially loved my Darth Vader doll.
They laughed at me; Darth was for boys,
the troubled ones, the kind of boys I gravitated
toward in life. The kind I would eventually
fall in love with.

They watched sitcoms. I read books.
They doodled. I painted.
They kept their dainty hands and fingers clean.
I got paint stuck in my hair and clay embedded
under my nails.
They got prim, tidy and pretty.
I got muddy, dirty and beautiful.
They learned to hide their flaws.
I learned to be proud of mine.

WITH PRETTY LEGS
Talin Tahajian

These are facts: I am part of that generation
that everyone seems to want more of.

This is no coincidence. *This one's for the girl
who just walked by / with the pretty legs.* Things

I have learned about myself: street musicians
love me. The girl at the coffee shop with all

those red tattoos. I am listing all of the people
who love me. Facts: Each day, at some point

between dawn & noon, I turn into a hawk.
A casual metamorphosis. There's something

about thunderstorms. More facts: I wake up
when the electricity comes back on. A family

of buzzing ghosts. They live in the dishwasher
& inside every warm lamp. This is all I know

about crystal balls. Seeing spirits. Animals dying
in the snow. *Love you, beautiful.* I am an animal

& someday I swear I'm going to die in this snow.
A sexy death with lots of wildfire smoke. *Hello*

beautiful. Moral: If I'm lucky, when the vultures
convene to love me, I will already be dead.

INSOMNIA

Jane Kenyon

The almost disturbing scent
of peonies presses through the screens,
and I know without looking how
those heavy white heads lean down
under the moon's light. A cricket chafes
and pauses, chafes and pauses,
as if distracted or preoccupied.

When I open my eyes to document
my sleeplessness by the clock, a point
of greenish light pulses near the ceiling.
A firefly . . . In childhood I ran out
at dusk, a jar in one hand, lid
pierced with airholes in the other,
getting soaked to the knees
in the long wet grass.

The light moves unsteadily, like someone
whose balance is uncertain after traveling
many hours, coming a long way.
Get up. Get up and let it out.

But I leave it hovering overhead, in case
it's my father, come back from the dead
to ask, "Why are you still awake? You can
put grass in their jar in the morning."

SELF-PORTRAITURE

Fariha Róisín

ONE
i am a self, yes
though sometimes it's hard
to believe
i am a body (troubled)
that I have one, too.

TWO
i count how to love myself, thoroughly,
an abacus, my love handles as armrests,
belly a scooped armchair,
a vulnerable asylum.

THREE
there's no choice, otherwise
the process is about letting yourself in
it's about loving gently, dearly
warm, a known embrace
rum coating the belly.

FOUR
all of me, awoken, and brown
like a sweet creature of defiance.

FIVE
i hate my weaknesses:
how people can hurt me
with one triumphant *just because.*

how i'm always small next to
others' self-assuredness
always—hand to heart—
waiting for a proffered description of *me*
to determine my worth.

i wait
for their approval to curl around my body,
a blanket of panicked
self-acceptance.

SIX
described as "too nice"
by the people closest.
sometimes i wear it like a badge, other times
like an ornate insult,
is everyone laughing at me?

SEVEN
my greed for love,
for my own perfection,
reeks of desperation,
but it is me and i am holy
in my unholiness, so
wonderfully messy,
that i can't help but begin
to win myself over.

EIGHT
i pour honey into
the ocean for Oshun.

NINE
the body's memory
more potent
more powerful
than human minds
than gendered egos.

i am alive,
and by god
i'm tired of being awakened, but unlived.
tomorrow, today, now

i step outside.

3 attitude

Call it boldness, grit, self-confidence. Poems can strut their stuff across the page, be fierce, poised, and fearless. What does Attitude look like? Feel like? Maya Angelou shows us "the fire in my eyes" and "the flash of my teeth" in "Phenomenal Woman." Ada Limón summons the "lady horse swagger" of a winning racehorse and feels the power of an "8-pound female horse heart" pumping inside her own body.

Attitude is unapologetic and full of appetite. It takes up space: "These hips are big hips," says Lucille Clifton. It says exactly what it wants: "I want to walk like I'm the only / woman on earth and I can have my pick," writes Kim Addonizio. As you read these poems, relish their determination. Find one that speaks your language and rhythms, and let its confidence inhabit you.

HOW TO TRIUMPH LIKE A GIRL
Ada Limón

I like the lady horses best,
how they make it all look easy,
like running 40 miles per hour
is as fun as taking a nap, or grass.
I like their lady horse swagger,
after winning. Ears up, girls, ears up!
But mainly, let's be honest, I like
that they're ladies. As if this big
dangerous animal is also a part of me,
that somewhere inside the delicate
skin of my body, there pumps
an 8-pound female horse heart,
giant with power, heavy with blood.
Don't you want to believe it?
Don't you want to lift my shirt and see
the huge beating genius machine
that thinks, no, it knows,
it's going to come in first.

BLACK DAUGHTER'S POINTILLISM

Amanda Gorman

I'm a piece of
Work. The mirror
Clears like a cloudy
Sky. In my temple, the
words brew. With a
pen I've
been both
the razed village
And the razor. Don't they know
I can stop a man's heart with one word? Write the future
Like I'm dragging my finger in wet sand? My every breath
A song carved out of the dark left behind? I've always been
A shadow of a girl,
Leaping behind a
Bonfire, trying to find
Its spark. Even in my quiet I
Gather stories like a sitting desk
Seeks dust. If I taste what I'm made of,
It's black as licorice. Ink. Fresh page of a new
Dawn. They will know me, and remember us: Girls
Who stitch these stories in the linings of our skirts so they hiss
In the satin folds as we strut towards freedom, throats clanging.
We bow, not cuz we broke, but as an oak bends, arching toward light.
In this faith, we wink and glimmer like a bright fist of glass, each of us a
Serrated piece
Of girl hard
At work

I'VE BEEN KNOWN

Denise Duhamel

to spread it on thick to shoot off my mouth to get it off my chest
    to tell him where
    to get off

to stay put to face the music to cut a shine to go under to sell
    myself short to play
    myself down

to paint the town to fork over to shell out to shoot up to pull a
    fast one to go haywire
    to take a shine to

to be stuck on to glam it up to vamp it up to get her one better to
    eat a little higher
    on the hog

to win out to get away with to go to the spot to make a stake to
    make a stand to
    stand for something to stand up for

to snow under to slip up to go for it to take a stab at it to try out
    to go places to play
    up to get back at

to size up to stand off to slop over to be solid with to lose my
    shirt to get myself off
    to get myself off the hook

HOMAGE TO MY HIPS

Lucille Clifton

these hips are big hips
they need space to
move around in.
they don't fit into little
petty places. these hips
are free hips.
they don't like to be held back.
these hips have never been enslaved,
they go where they want to go
they do what they want to do.
these hips are mighty hips.
these hips are magic hips.
i have known them
to put a spell on a man and
spin him like a top!

SHE PLAYS HOCKEY ON A BOYS' TEAM

Clara Bush Vadala

About the first of girls who wore the jock
without a cup to hold her hockey socks
up: You were perfect. When I saw your hair
unfold from helmet, I grew out mine, long

and blonde. I wanted some new hockey gear
because of you and got it. Brother's team
had openings. I signed up. Listen here,
I skated fast, was taller than the team

of boys before their prime. On ice with them
is where I learned to fight: you throw the gloves
but keep the helmet buckled. Boys will punch
whatever they can reach. By looking tough

a girl can win most any fight like this:
she keeps her head, boy breaks his fist.

IN CRITIQUE OF MODESTY

Angélica María Aguilera

"hey girl can we tone it down? less spanish, more sponsor
    friendly?
what if we change the words around? we would never
    want to offend anyone of course"

a professor says I ought to try a more modest approach
    to writing,
a potential employer says I ought to dress more modestly
    for the job

what a meek cheering squad that modesty has, I respond
what unenthused, half committed fans, I say,

me
I want to yell the way belligerent American men
do
I want to shoot my guns at the sky in honorship and scream
I want a festival in the streets
I want nationalism for being
yes yes yes
I want shirts with my own face on them,
I want to be a bikini on a blonde white girl,
I want schools to make children recite an allegiance to me
    each morning

I want horns and a parade
please don't forget the fireworks
I want a song, plastic glitter stars scattered all over the
        pavement
I want to wave to you from space
I want to be staked on the front of someone's pick up truck
Hoorah hoorah

what extraordinary freedom, what definite safety
to be seen everywhere

unafraid.

"WHAT DO WOMEN WANT?"
Kim Addonizio

I want a red dress.
I want it flimsy and cheap,
I want it too tight, I want to wear it
until someone tears it off me.
I want it sleeveless and backless,
this dress, so no one has to guess
what's underneath. I want to walk down
the street past Thrifty's and the hardware store
with all those keys glittering in the window,
past Mr. and Mrs. Wong selling day-old
donuts in their café, past the Guerra brothers
slinging pigs from the truck and onto the dolly,
hoisting the slick snouts over their shoulders.
I want to walk like I'm the only
woman on earth and I can have my pick.
I want that red dress bad.
I want it to confirm
your worst fears about me,
to show you how little I care about you
or anything except what
I want. When I find it, I'll pull that garment
from its hanger like I'm choosing a body
to carry me into this world, through
the birth-cries and the love-cries too,
and I'll wear it like bones, like skin,
it'll be the goddamned
dress they bury me in.

CONFESSION

Leila Chatti

*"Oh, I wish I had died before this and was in oblivion,
    forgotten."*
    —Mary giving birth, the Holy Qur'an

Truth be told, I like Mary a little better
when I imagine her like this, crouched
and cursing, a boy-God pushing on
her cervix (I like remembering
she had a cervix, her body ordinary
and so like mine), girl-sweat lacing
rivulets like veins in the sand,
her small hands on her knees
not doves but hands, gripping,
a palm pressed to her spine, fronds
whispering like voyeurs overhead—
(oh Mary, like a God, I too take pleasure
in knowing you were not all
holy, that ache could undo you
like a knot)—and, suffering,
I admire this girl who cared
for a moment not about God
or His plans but her own
distinct life, this fiercer Mary who'd disappear
if it saved her, who'd howl *to Hell*
with salvation if it meant this pain,
the blessed adolescent who squatted
indignant in a desert, bearing His child
like a secret she never wanted to hear.

PHENOMENAL WOMAN
Maya Angelou

Pretty women wonder where my secret lies.
I'm not cute or built to suit a fashion model's size
But when I start to tell them,
They think I'm telling lies.
I say,
It's in the reach of my arms,
The span of my hips,
The stride of my step,
The curl of my lips.
I'm a woman
Phenomenally.
Phenomenal woman,
That's me.

I walk into a room
Just as cool as you please,
And to a man,
The fellows stand or
Fall down on their knees.
Then they swarm around me,
A hive of honey bees.
I say,
It's the fire in my eyes,
And the flash of my teeth,
The swing in my waist,
And the joy in my feet.
I'm a woman
Phenomenally.

Phenomenal woman,
That's me.

Men themselves have wondered
What they see in me.
They try so much
But they can't touch
My inner mystery.
When I try to show them,
They say they still can't see.
I say,
It's in the arch of my back,
The sun of my smile,
The ride of my breasts,
The grace of my style.
I'm a woman
Phenomenally.
Phenomenal woman,
That's me.

Now you understand
Just why my head's not bowed.
I don't shout or jump about
Or have to talk real loud.
When you see me passing,
It ought to make you proud.
I say,

It's in the click of my heels,
The bend of my hair,
the palm of my hand,
The need for my care.
'Cause I'm a woman
Phenomenally.
Phenomenal woman,
That's me.

4 rage

Rage is storm and scream, raw anger multiplied and alchemized into power. This emotion is enormous and often contains frustration, resentment, aggression, betrayal, jealousy, helplessness, and hurt. For those of us who've been raised to "be nice," expressing rage is a vital release and can catalyze action, freeing us from the bonds of silence.

Sometimes, in poems, rage takes animal form: Aria Aber describes "this fury / at my center" in "Self-Portrait as Wounded Doe of Artemis." For Rage Hezekiah, anger is a kind of "armor," while for Bianca Stone it allows "self-preservation." Dominique Christina rages directly at a nameless misogynist on Twitter, lacerating him with her "anatomy lesson infused with feminist politics," which is transformed into a gorgeous ode to menstruation.

I hope that reading these poems will make you feel powerful, even invincible. Collectively, women's anger can be a galvanizing force. Let the poets' furor give you courage.

HARDER
Melissa Stein

If you're going to storm,
I said, do it harder.
Pummel nests from limbs
and drown the furred things
in their dens. Swell creek
to flood, unhome the fish.
Everything's gone too cozy.
Winnow, flush. Let's see
what's got the will.
Let's watch what's tender
choke or breathe. Try
to make a mark on me.

ON ANGER
Rage Hezekiah

My white therapist calls it my *edge*, I hear
Angry Black Woman. She says, *Strength
of Willful Negative Focus.* She says, *Acerbic
Intellectual Temperament.* I copy her words
onto an index card. She wants
an origin story, a stranger with his hand
inside me, or worse. I'm without
linear narrative and cannot sate her. We
perform rituals on her living room floor. I burn
letters brimming with resentments, watch
the paper ember in the fireplace, admit
I don't want to let this go. What if anger,
my armor, is embedded in the marrow
of who I am. Who can I learn to be
without it? *Wherever you go,
there you are.* She asks what I will lose
if I surrender, I imagine a gutted fish,
silvery skin gleaming, emptied of itself—

THE PERIOD POEM

Dominique Christina

Dude on twitter said:

"I was having sex with my girlfriend when
she started her period.
I dumped that bitch immediately."

Dear nameless dummy on Twitter:

You're the reason my daughter cried funeral tears
When she started her period.
The sudden grief all young girls feel
After the matriculation from childhood and
The induction into a reality that they'll have to negotiate
People like you and your disdain
For what a woman's body can do.

Herein begins an anatomy lesson infused with feminist politics
Because I hate you.

There's a thing . . . called a uterus.
It sheds itself every 28 days or so
Or in my case every 23 days
(I've always been a rule breaker).

I digress.

That's the anatomy part.

The feminist politic part is that women
Know how to let things go,
How to let a dying thing leave the body,
How to become new,
How to regenerate,
How to wax and wane not unlike the moon and tides,
Both of which influence how YOU behave.

I digress.

Women have vaginas that can speak to each other.
By this I mean, when we're with our friends,
Our sisters, our mothers,
Our menstrual cycles will actually sync the fuck up.
My own vagina is mad influential.
Everybody I love knows how to bleed with me.
(Hold onto that, there's a metaphor in it).

But when your mother carried you,
The ocean in her belly is what made you buoyant,
Made you possible.
You had it under your tongue when you burst through her skin,
Wet and panting from the heat of her body,
The body whose machinery you now mock on social media,

THAT body wrapped you in everything
That was miraculous about it and sang you
Lullabies laced in platelets
Without which you wouldn't have a twitter account
At all, motherfucker.

I digress.

See, it's possible we know the world better
Because of the blood that visits some of us.
It interrupts our favorite white skirts and
Shows up at dinner parties unannounced.

Blood will do that.

Period.

It will come when you're not prepared for it.

Blood does that.

Period.

Blood's the biggest siren and
We understand that blood misbehaves.
It doesn't wait for a hand signal or a
Welcome sign above the door.

And when you deal in blood
Over and over again like we do,
When it keeps returning to you,
That makes you a warrior and
While all good generals know not to discuss
Battle plans with the enemy
Let me say this to you, dummy on Twitter:
If there's any balance in the universe at all . . .
You'll be blessed with daughters.

Blessed.

Etymologically "Bless" means: to make bleed.
See? Now it's a lesson in linguistics.
In other words blood speaks.
That's the message.
Stay with me.

Your daughters will teach you
What all men must one day come to know,
That women, made of moonlight, magic, and macabre,
Will make you know the blood.
We'll get it all over the sheets and car seats.

We'll do that.
We introduce you to our insides.

Period.

And if you're as unprepared as we sometimes are,
It'll get all over you and leave a forever stain.

So, to my daughter:

Should any fool mishandle
The wild geography of your body,
How it rides a red running current,
Like any good wolf, or witch, well then . . .

Just BLEED.

Give that blood a Biblical name,
Something of stone and mortar.
Name it after Eve's first rebellion in that garden.
Name it after the last little girl to have her genitals
Mutilated in Kinshasa (that was this morning),
Give it as many syllables as there are unreported rape cases.

Name the blood something holy.
Something mighty.
Something un-languageable.
Something in hieroglyphs.
Something that sounds like the end of the world.

Name it for the roar between your legs and
For the women who'll not be nameless here.

Just bleed anyhow.

Spill your impossible scripture
All over the good furniture.

Bleed and bleed and bleed

On EVERYTHING he loves . . . period.

AND IF BY INVISIBILITY
Tamiko Beyer

they mean they do not see us
our bows and gnashing teeth
our prom dress feather boa heels
hair glittered gray the fisting and holler
fishnets fishnets breasts breasts breasts
our voices pitched forward into reclamation
the blood in our mouths sweet slick
like our ready-to-take-you between our legs —
we signify no shelter signify
the precipice from where we've returned
all our baskets full of fruit and shark teeth
in the end no vision villain-split
our diy manicures all silvery and chipped
our shouts so lovely so lovely all that licking

ONES WHO GOT AWAY WITH IT

Bianca Stone

I still fantasize I can do something about it.
That girl in the outpatient-care-facility for teenagers
confided to me that she sneaked out to see a guy
at his frat party, and he *shared* her with his three friends,
to have a taste after he was done. "Is it supposed
to hurt so much?" she whispered to me. "I mean,
for this long *after*?" She was bulimic, and we both
hated our mothers. The next day I said, *We should
tell someone.* And she said, "I've talked it over
with my best friend. She says
I should be proud of it." She was thirteen
and I, sixteen, recovering from those endless nights of shrieking
across the house, out into the yard and
into the cold moonlight to wish myself into some
other species; the endless silent Stooges' bangs and thwacks,
some self-preservation up against inherited solitude;
bent almost in half, the copper piping of my family grief
that always raked itself across me
until I was deformed by it,
until I was defined by it—
but dammit,
                    I hope that girl's doing well.
I hope she can keep down food
and it's nourishing her. I hope her cells are cheering
like parents in the stands at a game, even if those men still exist—
important men, I imagine. Men who now run conglomerates

and have well-to-do families. Or maybe men I see
every day at work. Or whose books I read.

And how am I here? With my life intact?
I'm painful to the touch only when I don't light
a candle and praise oblivion, give myself over
to nothingness—and is it every day
or was it long ago,
that I'd slid shut my teenage self's veranda doors
and stepped
onto the world's fancy balconies
and was prepared to do something drastic
like live and live and live.

REHEARSAL
Sara Peters

I am walking through water with one of my sisters,
   the river banked with tiger lilies, the sun
like having a lemon juiced into your eye, our senile dog

ecstatic behind us,
   and I am yammering
about my discovery—

a chest deep pool, sentried by trees
   that caterpillars were killing
with their yearly carnival tents.

We reach then ruin the pool with oils and shampoos.
   We scrub too much skin
from our heels, then debate

whether to sunbathe naked:
   that is, who is hiding in the woods.
We joke so long and rough

the joke morphs, till we're practicing for
   our future rapes:
we both have numbers that we know are up.

My sister's ears are speared
   with porcupine quills and steel,
but she's placed her straw hat carefully over her stomach.

As she talks I watch
        while dragonflies and other
less showy insects land

on her burning shoulders.
        The dragonflies present their stenciled wings.
I can't remember what the others do.

My sister spits
        to clean each sunglass mirror.
She wants me to hear

how, when it happens,
        she'll do this scream—
but when the scream comes it's just like she's opened

a shaken bottle of sparkling water:
        I am speechless only for the view
of her throat's cushioned corridor.

But when the scream ends her eyes
        have broken off from the rest of her face.
She takes our green net bag full of oranges,

and slams it down on the baking rocks,
        beating the ground till the oranges soften
and streak the air with the smell of their breaking.

SELF-PORTRAIT AS WOUNDED DOE OF ARTEMIS

Aria Aber

I wake up
pollarded by desire
to see jawbreakers city-scuttling,

to rage among halva wrappers,
diamorphine sparkling
across the night-womb.

I need to assuage this fury
at my center:
poppies tether me

to the soil, while on my forehead
the ghost of horns
blisters into scurs:

myrrh, orange blossom, lamb
kebab. All I have now
is naked, rubies

rotting my head—
I am the worst
girl I can be,

galloping, an invisible screech:
inside my body's
untamable

meadow, a herd
of selves soughs
to expose itself.

Fur and itch—
under my dress of rods
I'm armored,

hot and ready to pierce
into Zeus—but he has
lonelied this city

now, so I perforate
his trembling cats, the elders.
Stop me.

Split me. Yes,
once I was frail
with holy, a handful

of pistachio shells
breaking under
my heel—now I'm too much

to handle, a rocking
sound, an un-wine-dark
pooling around me.

And the pale hands that sink
into my hindlimbs
pluck a kalimba:

sweat, buttermilk,
a colossal chirr.
I am fingered like dirt,

a hothouse of plums—
and I break open
like the country I come from.

SELF-PORTRAIT AS MANGO

Tarfia Faizullah

She says, *Your English is great! How long have you been in our country?*
I say, *Suck on a mango, bitch,* since that's all you think I eat anyway. Mangoes

are what margins like me know everything about, right? Doesn't
a mango just win spelling bees and kiss white boys? Isn't a mango

a placeholder in a poem folded with burkas? But this one,
the one I'm going to slice and serve down her throat, is a mango

that remembers jungles jagged with insects, the river's darker thirst.
This mango was cut down by a scythe that beheads soldiers, mango

that taunts and suns itself into a hard-palmed fist only a few months
per year, fattens while blood stains green ponds. Why use a mango

to beat her perplexed? Why not a coconut? Because this "exotic" fruit
won't be cracked open to reveal whiteness to you. This mango

isn't alien just because of its gold-green bloodline. I know
I'm worth waiting for. I want to be kneaded for ripeness. Mango:

my own sunset-skinned heart waiting to be held and peeled, mango
I suck open with teeth. *Tappai!* This is the only way to eat a mango.

5 longing

Longing can be delicious or painful, intense or dreamy, or sometimes all these things at once. It encompasses sparks, crushes, chemistry, passion, a yearning for connection. One of the most potent human emotions, longing is often a source of energy and creativity.

Marie Howe reveals "the first pure thrill of unreluctant desire" at seventh-grade sleepovers. In "coming of age," Evie Shockley relishes the superstar Prince and his "sweetly relentless" pop songs, how they embodied longing for her thirteen-year-old self. And Michelle Tea captures the push/pull of it: "that exhausted walk to reach you / breathless."

Longing can also be for friendship, as in Holly Burdorff's "Song to Elise," which recalls the freedom of childhood. And it may not always be for another person, but for a voice, for justice, for meaning, for self-expression. Cameron Awkward-Rich dreams of a world without borders or suffering. Sharon Olds longs to return to the past and change her parents, her family history. She concludes the poem in triumph, claiming her own storytelling power: "Do what you are going to do, and I will tell about it."

FAST GAS

Dorianne Laux

for Richard

Before the days of self service,
when you never had to pump your own gas,
I was the one who did it for you, the girl
who stepped out at the sound of a bell
with a blue rag in my hand, my hair pulled back
in a straight, unlovely ponytail.
This was before automatic shut-offs
and vapor seals, and once, while filling a tank,
I hit a bubble of trapped air and the gas
backed up, came arcing out of the hole
in a bright gold wave and soaked me—face, breasts,
belly and legs. And I had to hurry
back to the booth, the small employee bathroom
with the broken lock, to change my uniform,
peel the gas-soaked cloth from my skin
and wash myself in the sink.
Light-headed, scrubbed raw, I felt
pure and amazed—the way the amber gas
glazed my flesh, the searing,
subterranean pain of it, how my skin
shimmered and ached, glowed
like rainbowed oil on the pavement.

I was twenty. In a few weeks I would fall,
for the first time, in love, that man waiting
patiently in my future like a red leaf
on the sidewalk, the kind of beauty
that asks to be noticed. How was I to know
it would begin this way: every cell of my body
burning with a dangerous beauty, the air around me
a nimbus of light that would carry me
through the days, how when he found me,
weeks later, he would find me like that,
an ordinary woman who could rise
in flame, all he would have to do
is come close and touch me.

PRACTICING
Marie Howe

I want to write a love poem for the girls I kissed in seventh grade,
a song for what we did on the floor in the basement

of somebody's parents' house, a hymn for what we didn't say but thought:
That feels good or *I like that*, when we learned how to open each other's mouths

how to move our tongues to make somebody moan. We called it practicing, and
one was the boy, and we paired off—maybe six or eight girls—and turned out

the lights and kissed and kissed until we were stoned on kisses, and lifted our
nightgowns or let the straps drop, and, Now you be the boy:

concrete floor, sleeping bag or couch, playroom, game room, train room, laundry.
Linda's basement was like a boat with booths and portholes

instead of windows. Gloria's father had a bar downstairs with stools that spun, plush carpeting. We kissed each other's throats.

We sucked each other's breasts, and we left marks, and never spoke of it upstairs outdoors, in daylight, not once. We did it, and it was

practicing, and slept, sprawled so our legs still locked or crossed, a hand still lost in someone's hair . . . and we grew up and hardly mentioned who

the first kiss really was—a girl like us, still sticky with moisturizer we'd shared in the bathroom. I want to write a song

for that thick silence in the dark, and the first pure thrill of unreluctant desire, just before we made ourselves stop.

MEDITATIONS IN AN EMERGENCY
Cameron Awkward-Rich

I wake up & it breaks my heart. I draw the blinds
& the thrill of rain breaks my heart. I go outside.
I ride the train, walk among the buildings, men in
Monday suits. The flight of doves, the city of tents
beneath the underpass, the huddled mass, old
women hawking roses, & children all of them,
break my heart. There's a dream I have in which I
love the world. I run from end to end like fingers
through her hair. There are no borders, only wind.
Like you, I was born. Like you, I was raised in the
institution of dreaming. Hand on my heart. Hand
on my stupid heart.

OH GOD

Michelle Tea

spilling water from my back,
you call and i come.
that exhausted walk to reach you
breathless and no i didn't run
to see you, i've been smoking
too much, same thing.

another awkward hug in the car
as my face smashes your cheek
that i can feel it leaving now
is the saddest, a beautiful eruption
you could have picked it off the tree
and chowed

but you weren't hungry.
feeling it dying away all day
much worse than the straining
against the leash, another gorgeous
thing that should not have happened,
gone again.

ON THE DISCOMFORT OF BEING IN THE SAME ROOM AS THE BOY YOU LIKE

Sarah Kay

Everyone is looking at you looking at him.
Everyone can tell. *He can tell.* So you
spend most of your time not looking at him.
The wallpaper, the floor, there are cracks
in the ceiling. Someone has left a can of
iced tea in the corner, it is half-empty,
I mean half-full. There are four light bulbs
in the standing lamp, there is a fan. You
are counting things to keep from looking
at him. Five chairs, two laptops, someone's
umbrella, a hat. People are talking so you
look at their faces. This is a good trick. They
will think you are listening to them and not
thinking about him. Now he is talking. So
you look away. The cracks in the ceiling are
in the shape of a whale or maybe an elephant
with a fat trunk. If he ever falls in love with
you, you will lie on your backs in a field
somewhere and look up at the sky and he will
say, *Baby, look at that silly cloud, it is a whale!*
and you will say, *Baby, that is an elephant
with a fat trunk*, and you will argue for a bit,
but he will love you anyway.

He is asking a question now and no one has answered it yet. So you lower your eyes from the plaster and say, *the twenty first, I think,* and he smiles and says, *oh, cool,* and you smile back, and you cannot stop your smiling, oh you cannot stop your smile.

COMING OF AGE
Evie Shockley

until i turned thirteen   until that afternoon in

the locker room when i heard you sing soft *and wet* from beginning to

end   so sweetly relentless i forgot to be shy about the half-nakedness

of my awkwarding body   paused with musky gym shorts in hand while

time slipped into your drum machine   and rivered over your keyboards

i'll bet i'd never heard a boy

be so damn   accurate   about the state of my titillation   and be cause

there was your voice   cream   to dive into   to ladle out in long thin threads

for   (purple doves   i wanna be delirious)

you   (little red kiss   if i was your erotic city)

you sang   for me   for us   the holy promise of your shadowed eyes was my
own and my best friend's daily church   long phone calls from darkened rooms
my *head* between your hi-fi croon and her whisper   we sang   for   the whole
heart of our friendship pulsed with   *do me, baby*   with   *still waiting*
and why we needed to see   be   the reflection of your dirty
mind in   for   each other   for all those hot years

i still do not know   we talked of other boys   learning how desires of   for
truly woman bodies could be spoken   from a man's falsetto   what it is to
adore sex   a prayer for flesh to meet flesh like a thundercloud   *soft*
you sang   and sing still today in my own and my lover's skin   *and wet*

WANTING IT

Diana Whitney

Wasn't I beautiful, wasn't I desperate,
didn't I give a shit about world peace, inner peace,
only wanting it, wanting it, secret graffiti

spelled out in lip gloss on the locker-room wall?

The new underwire bit into my ribs, pushed
me up and I caught the mirror, wanted it, cocked a hip,
wanted it—front seat, back seat,

down on the floor, brag of bruises
blooming like plums on my neck, tender,
bad and legitimate. I wanted

to ditch it, wanted to drive, alone

in the car for the first time, silence, such
concentration my hands tongued the wheel. I could see
the brush-stroke of each yellow line, could feel

my tires crush pieces of gravel, and my ten toes
alive inside my shoes, firm and quick
on the pedals. There was an orange

lodged underneath the clutch. Squeeze it and shift,
squeeze it and *there*. Those boys

who juiced the halls with slouch
and threw their bodies around the field—they watched
when I punched it to second, third, burned my tracks

along the high school tar. They looked at me
as if I could kill them. They wanted to kill me
back against a locker. I could feel

my body jammed up on metal, my skin
in ridges where the grates dug in,

my skirt hiked up, my muscles like fish,
my third eye watching from the outside in.

I was some other girl.
I was anyone's candy.

SONG TO ELISE

Holly Burdorff

Before high school,
before we shaved our legs,
before we spent our nights
passing fries out drive-thru windows,
your mother and mine cleaned offices
at the zoo in Cleveland.
On Saturdays, they'd whisk you and me
in for free through the service entrance,
slip violet chiffon sack dresses over our heads,
   "to find you easier in the closing crowd."

We'd spend summer days racing
through your back cornfield,
the stalks scratching our ankles,
calves, then our thighs. Bare feet,
yellow sundresses, tangled hair flying
in the wind. We'd squeeze between the bars
of the mud-stuck back truck gate
toward the maple tree grove
connecting our properties. We hung ropes
and swung on whichever branches
would hold our weight.

I know your daddy's in jail now,
and that's a lot of bull to bear.
Since you moved back to the city
I haven't swung on any trees.
But sometimes I loop my fingers around my eyes
and think of how you'd climb to the top limb,
slip on your daddy's reading glasses,
and tell me stories of the clouds in the sky.

BUT THEY SAY I WILL NOT MAKE IT

Rachel Wiley

When you are fat (and I am fat) the streets are full of
soothsayers
telling you how you will die.
    They all seem so anxious for my heart
    like it's an unattended package at the airport
  so I move thru the world listening
    for my heart like it must be a clock
      swallowed by a crocodile.
              No,
       a canary that goes silent much too late.
          No,
they are certain it is going to attack, my heart,
    like a hungry bear on a camp ground
      ripping a zipper down my chest, cracking
    my sternum like a cheap tent pole.
          No,
    I am not at all sorry for my size
  so I must be a barge which would make my heart a fish
      washed onto the deck
    GaspingFloppingSlamming scales off its body
like an angry beauty queen ripping sequins from a dress
    that didn't sparkle enough to win
  but then that would make my heart a beauty queen
that can't walk in heels . . .
        No,
         wait.

My heart is an hourglass filled with gunpowder
and at any given moment some wild spark
        is gonna blow me sky high
so, I don't know, maybe this is why I love the way I do
with teeth and swallow and song and snarl
        and water and sparkle and consequence
maybe this is why I show up to your front door
        out of breath and full of dazzle
            like this is the last ballyhoo
and nothing at all can wait till the morning.

Forgive me, they keep telling me that my heart is not my heart.
They keep telling me that I am dying.
This may be our last chance.

I GO BACK TO MAY 1937

Sharon Olds

I see them standing at the formal gates of their colleges,
I see my father strolling out
under the ochre sandstone arch, the
red tiles glinting like bent
plates of blood behind his head, I
see my mother with a few light books at her hip
standing at the pillar made of tiny bricks,
the wrought-iron gate still open behind her, its
sword-tips aglow in the May air,
they are about to graduate, they are about to get married,
they are kids, they are dumb, all they know is they are
innocent, they would never hurt anybody.
I want to go up to them and say Stop,
don't do it—she's the wrong woman,
he's the wrong man, you are going to do things
you cannot imagine you would ever do,
you are going to do bad things to children,
you are going to suffer in ways you have not heard of,
you are going to want to die. I want to go
up to them there in the late May sunlight and say it,
her hungry pretty face turning to me,
her pitiful beautiful untouched body,
his arrogant handsome face turning to me,
his pitiful beautiful untouched body,

but I don't do it. I want to live. I
take them up like the male and female
paper dolls and bang them together
at the hips, like chips of flint, as if to
strike sparks from them, I say
Do what you are going to do, and I will tell about it.

6 shame

Every girl knows about shame, the belief that we are not enough, that we're flawed somehow at our very core. It's a feeling of being unworthy of love, damaged beyond repair. A shame spiral can be acutely painful, trapping us in fear, humiliation, self-consciousness, and self-loathing.

Writer Brené Brown says that guilt is the feeling you've *done* something wrong, whereas shame is the belief that you yourself *are* wrong. I remember the anguish of middle school: crying in the fluorescent glare of a T. J. Maxx dressing room, cringing at my flesh in a pink bikini. It was shame that inhabited me after my sexual assault at eighteen, whispering that I deserved this violation.

But when we talk about shame, it lessens. And when we read the poets, they offer compassion. Blythe Baird confesses her eating disorder: "hunching naked over a bathroom scale shrine." Natalie Diaz recalls hunger and poverty, the sense of being "devoured by shame."

It's shame that makes us apologize for ourselves—for our bodies, our stories, and our "wild" (as Nikita Gill calls it). But the poets promise the reprieve of creativity. We can use our voices. We can realize that the shame others have invented for us is false—as Lynn Melnick discovers in her poem—and refuse to carry it anymore.

ODE TO GOSSIPS
Safia Elhillo

i was mothered by lonely women   some
of them wives   some of them   with

plumes of smoke for husbands   all lonely
smelling of onions & milk   all mothers

some of them to children some to old names
phantom girls acting out a life   only half

a life away   instead   copper kitchenware
bangles pushed up the arm   fingernails rusted

with henna   kneading raw meat with salt
with coriander   sweating upper lip

in the steam   weak tea   hair unwound
against the nape   my deities   each one

sandal slapping against stone heel   sandal-
wood & oud   bright chiffon spun

about each head   coffee in the dowry china
butter biscuits on a painted plate   crumbs

suspended in eggshell demitasse   & they
begin   *i heard*   *people are saying*

i saw it with my own eyes   [   ]'s daughter
a scandal   *she was wearing [   ]*

& not wearing [   ]   can you imagine
a shame   *a shame*

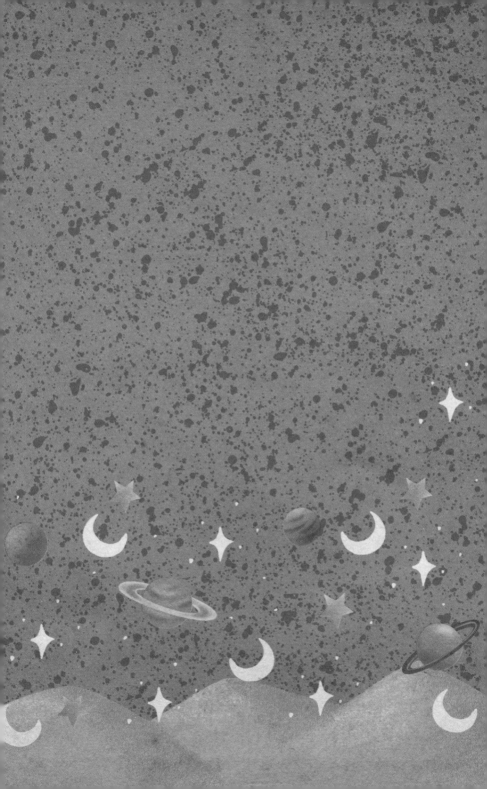

WOLF AND WOMAN
Nikita Gill

Some days
I am more wolf
than woman
and I am still learning
how to stop apologizing
for my wild.

SONNET FOR A DOLLAR

Natalie Scenters-Zapico

You tied the boy's shoes every morning.
You washed his desk with shaving cream.
You opened your mouth & let him look inside.
You kicked teacher in the shin & said: *Sorry, Miss.*

You kissed him on the lips for five seconds.
You gave him shivers. You gave him the knife.
You read books in a whisper, close to his face.
You let him slap you, then rock you in his arms.

You let him unclasp your bra with his eyes closed.
You let him call you puta in front of his friends.
You let him bite your finger until it turned purple.
You crawled on your hands & knees like a dog.

When you told your father all the things you'd done
for a dollar, he laughed & laughed.

WHY I HATE RAISINS
Natalie Diaz

And is it only the mouth and belly which are
injured by hunger and thirst?
Mencius

Love is a pound of sticky raisins
packed tight in black and white
government boxes the day we had no
groceries. I told my mom I was hungry.
She gave me the whole bright box.
USDA stamped like a fist on the side.
I ate them all in ten minutes. Ate
too many too fast. It wasn't long
before those old grapes set like black
clay at the bottom of my belly
making it ache and swell.

I complained, *I hate raisins.*
I just wanted a sandwich like other kids.
Well that's all we've got, my mom sighed.
And what other kids?
Everyone but me, I told her.
She said, *You mean the white kids.*
You want to be a white kid?
Well too bad 'cause you're my kid.
I cried, *At least the white kids get a sandwich.*
At least the white kids don't get the shits.

That's when she slapped me. Left me
holding my mouth and stomach—
devoured by shame.
I still hate raisins,
but not for the crooked commodity lines
we stood in to get them—winding
around and in the tribal gymnasium.
Not for the awkward cardboard boxes
we carried them home in. Not for the shits
or how they distended my belly.
I hate raisins because now I know
my mom was hungry that day, too,
and I ate all the raisins.

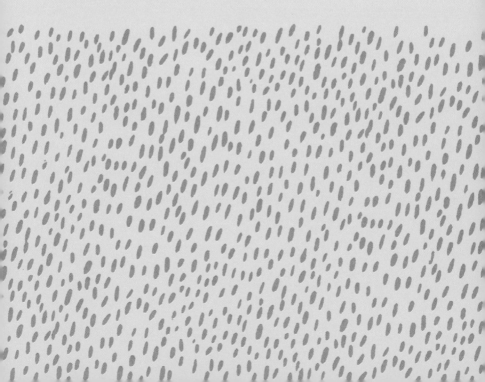

WHEN THE FAT GIRL GETS SKINNY

Blythe Baird

the year of skinny pop and sugar-free jello cups
we guzzled vitamin water and vodka

toasting to high school and survival
complimenting each other's collarbones

trying diets we found on the internet:
menthol cigarettes, eating in front of a mirror,

donating blood

replacing meals with other practical hobbies
like making flower crowns

or fainting

wondering why I haven't had my period
in months

why breakfast tastes like
giving up

or how many more productive ways
I could have spent my time today

besides googling the calories
in the glue of a US envelope,

watching *America's Next Top Model*
like the gospel,

hunching naked over a bathroom scale shrine,
crying into an empty bowl of Cocoa Puffs

because I only feel pretty
when I'm hungry

if you are not recovering
you are dying

by the time I was sixteen, I had already experienced
being clinically overweight, underweight, and obese

as a child, *fat* was the first word
people used to describe me

which didn't offend me until
I found out it was supposed to

when I lost weight, my dad was so proud
he started carrying my before-and-after photo

in his wallet

so relieved he could stop worrying
about me getting diabetes

he saw a program on the news
about the epidemic with obesity,

says he is *just so glad* to finally see me
taking care of myself

if you develop an eating disorder
when you are already thin to begin with,

you go to the hospital

if you develop an eating disorder
when you are not thin to begin with,

you are a success story

so when I evaporated, of course
everyone congratulated me

on getting healthy

girls at school who never spoke to me before
stopped me in the hallway to ask how I did it

I say, *I am sick*
they say, *No, you are*

an inspiration

how could I not fall
in love with my illness?

with becoming the kind of silhouette
people are supposed to fall in love with?

why would I ever want to stop
being hungry

when anorexia was the most
interesting thing about me?

so, how lucky it is now,
to be boring

the way not going to the hospital
is boring

the way looking at an apple
and seeing only an apple, not sixty

or half an hour of sit-ups
is boring

my story may not be as exciting as it used
to be, but at least there is nothing left

to count

the calculator in my head
finally stopped

I used to love the feeling of drinking water
on an empty stomach

waiting for the coolness to slip all
the way down and land in the well

not obsessed with being empty
but afraid of being full

I used to take pride in being able to feel
cold in a warm room

now, I am proud I have stopped
seeking revenge on this body

this was the year of eating
when I was hungry

without punishing myself

and I know it sounds ridiculous
but that shit is hard

when I was little,
someone asked me

what I wanted to be
when I grew up

and I said,

small

THE MOCKERS

Mary Meriam

What rich glass bottle held the picture of
our music teacher, name I can't recall.
I only know I had a twisted love
for her, that she was strange, alone, and tall.
We took the bottle to the field out back,
my childhood friend and I, and dug a grave.
Whatever crazy words we said, I lack
them now. Or did we sing or laugh, I crave
this memory, our kneeling on the ground
one afternoon to place Miss X in earth.
I strain my mind with hope to hear a sound,
even a bird, or leaves in wind, what birth
of folly or regret was brewing then,
what digging up could bring her back again.

"IS THERE SOMETHING I SHOULD KNOW?"*

Brenda Shaughnessy

If a girl was good enough, and pretty enough, sexy
in the way that could earn the right kind of attention,

she might attract a guy who treated her special,
as a complicated and exciting human being who

just happened to be sexy in the way that could
earn this right kind of attention.

This was the goal of the game.
This game with the vibe of a Roman gladiator stadium.

It was real life, this game, but you still had to play it.
If you won, you got to keep your body.

If you lost, you lost everything: your confidence,
your easy laughter, your ability to look in the mirror

and feel beautiful, your secret language, your eros,
your sense of humor, your flamboyant clothing style,

your enthusiasm for side-projects or for developing
your weaker arts, your lust, your late nights

alone without fear, your trust, your tipsy nights
dancing with friends, your friendships, your grades,

your way of flirting, your strange ability to shoot milk
out of your nose if there is sufficient social pressure,

your scholarship, your self-respect, your kindness,
your nights without nightmares, your openness,

your sense that you could choose or do what you wanted
and loved to do, your all and your future all.

Your dreams of having desire, believing that could
be relevant, and of fooling around, getting excited,

maybe falling for someone and wanting them,
and being wanted without being used by someone

who knows exactly how to use you.
Your story. The book of your life,

just the way you wanted to tell it, in the full
range of your voice.

excerpt

LANDSCAPE WITH CLINIC AND ORACLE

Lynn Melnick

Maybe you're not the featherweight champ
of all the cutthroat combat sports

(fifteen and pregnant
again)

but you'd convert your ring corner
into a slaughterhouse

before you'd inquire after human kindness.

In the humdrum flare outside the clinic
you wait for a ride, feel the spill at the tipping point

trickle down your inner thigh
as you bask in the post-industrial particulate

on your skin, ash
into a jasmine pot's bituminous anchorage

so tacky it glows in a habitat that spent your body
long before it finished growing.

      Lynn! they lied to you

don't you know?
Your womb will be the first thing to heal.

What you smell is pleasure, not the rot of the thing
amid the waste.

You will have babies.
You will write poems about flowers that turn on in darkness.

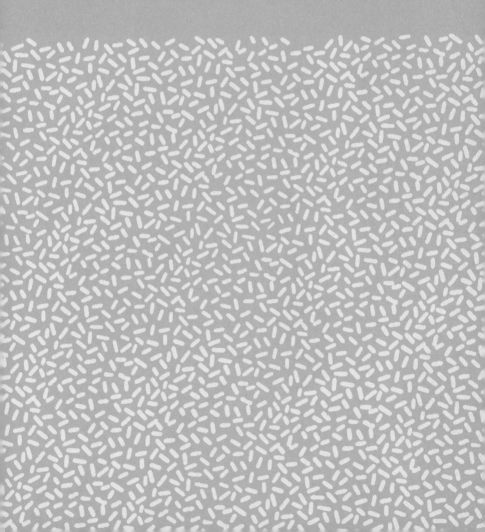

7 | sadness

Sadness casts a deep net, encompassing heartbreak, despair, depression, emptiness, misery, homesickness, and grief. But the poets console us that we are not alone in our sadness. They show us how to use it, transmute it, bear the weight by speaking it aloud.

M. J. Fievre describes her depression as "a chill that settles inside me, / a marrow-deep tremor." She discovers her own strong legs through the process of writing the poem. Alison Prine captures the shape-shifting, cyclical nature of grief in "Rearview Mirror: February," an elegy for her mother that reminds me how much I miss my own dad, gone fifteen years now. Reading her poem gave me a good kind of hurt, the gift of being seen.

These poets get right up close to sadness. They show us how to let ourselves feel it. Alison C. Rollins opens "the book of trauma" and finds resilience. JP Howard comforts a friend who wants to give up with the solace of tears, breath, and warm skin. These writers promise that sorrow always shifts and pain becomes bearable, like Crystal Williams's gentle blessing in "Night Bloom":

> *If you cannot believe that things will soften*
> *trust that I believe for you.*

WHAT TO SAY TO A FRIEND WHO WANTS TO GIVE UP

JP Howard

Say I love you, even when you can't love yourself.
Say please, please not today,
Say too much life unlived.
Say mirror, say beautiful,
Say this arm, take this arm,
Say grab, say hold, say let tears fall,
Say tears heal, Say forgive your mama,
Say she did the best she could.
Say tomorrow, say sleep,
Say split second, split the seconds,
Say let the seconds turn into days,
Say today, Say tomorrow, Say sun.
Say warm, Say skin,
Say warm skin, say sunlight,
Say new day, Say breathe,
Say inhale, Say exhale.
Say not today baby girl,
Say so much life to live,
Say love, Say I love you.
Say hold on, hold on to love.

REARVIEW MIRROR: FEBRUARY

Alison Prine

My beginning and your ending got so close
that all traces of you in my memory
lost hold.

When I have nothing left to say,
I have you—
a series of disappearances,
a street sign, a shade of turquoise,
and a Formica table.

A few decades later
we have hundreds of sadness medications.
There is an information machine
in everyone's pocket.

We have nothing left to say,
and we keep saying it.

Take my face between your hands.
Is this what you expected?
I thought I would write this once,
and instead
it is every time.

SKINNING GHOSTS ALIVE

Alison C. Rollins

In the beginning, there is no yes.
The amniotic sac a dust jacket

for the book of trauma. One plus one makes one.
There is a nomenclature to this math, a method

to the madness of creation. There is no he.
There is no she. There's just a girl expelling

Y from her loose-jowled maw. The residue of jargon
stains her lips boy-red. We are never our own.

This is why we are so lonely. Why light-headed stars
nestle their knives in the sky's black chest. Why we

eat men like air. Moon's bulb shaved down to a hang-
nail's comma. Straight as the line that reads you

your missing period and the knowing that this cannot
be allowed to continue. This belly not permitted

to raise a question. Even lightning shakes the earth
like a daughter. Who am I to object? Point fingers at the order.

//

I was born bad. A trail of yeses parading round
my hip's border. A trail of forget-me-nots sprouting
from my father's chin. This tongue needs shepherding,
as do these bones. I clench and carry the pain of my mother
in my teeth, at the root a canal of fear. The space between

each molar the size of the closet my grandmother's mother
locked her in as she cried *no* promising that she
would be good. So naturally my mouth's second nature is
naughty. This is how you end up leading the shell of a man
to your bed. How you crack your peanut-colored self
until the sidewalks of your cheeks are caked with salt.
Your lover's eyelids half-lit houses—terror veins its way
down the stairs. It is cold in this thing we call a body.
Who will tend to the fire with so few hands to go around?

//

Even a snake loses itself in its skin.
Its life's throat peeled back in molting song.

A second me lies somewhere on the ground.
Hollowed as the cicada shells I collected in the woods

as a child. Knowing then that the anatomy of loss
was worth picking, if only to acknowledge that

something has shed and not died, something brown as me
has left its skeleton behind, more intact than broken,

as if to say we are living
and dying just the same.

This is why we are so homesick,
why we hull ourselves in shadows.

EVENT HORIZON
Leslie Marie Aguilar

I am a body of light jettisoned through the universe at speeds beyond comprehension—a supernova afraid to be reborn. My illness is invisible this way. A system of shrinking. One day at a time. I signal for help from a deity that does not know my name, only the cadence of sighs. Afraid of failure, I exhale deeply. Travel from one satellite to another looking for a more expedient method of dissipating.

Some days this imagining is enough, but not the day I lose my wallet in a Wal-Mart parking lot, or the day I spend my life savings on an accent chair. How many times can I repeat, *everything will be okay*, & hope for a miracle in a moving van? It's selfish to be this unhappy, I think. But I can't imagine a better way of collapsing, except slowly, & then all at once.

WHAT YOU MOURN

Sheila Black

The year they straightened my legs,
the young doctor said, meaning to be kind,
Now you will walk straight
on your wedding day, but what he could not
imagine is how even on my wedding day
I would arch back and wonder
about that body I had before I was changed,
how I would have nested in it,
made it my home, how I repeated his words
when I wished to stir up my native anger
feel like the exile I believed
I was, imprisoned in a foreign body
like a person imprisoned in a foreign land
forced to speak a strange tongue
heavy in the mouth, a mouth full of stones.

Crippled they called us when I was young
later the word was *disabled* and then *differently abled*,
but those were all names given by outsiders,
none of whom could imagine
that the crooked body they spoke of,
the body, which made walking difficult
and running practically impossible,
except as a kind of dance, a sideways looping
like someone about to fall
headlong down and hug the earth, that body
they tried so hard to fix, straighten was simply mine,
and I loved it as you love your own country,

the familiar lay of the land, the unkempt trees,
the smell of mowed grass, down to the nameless
flowers at your feet—clover, asphodel,
and the blue flies that buzz over them.

NO FILTER

Andrea Gibson

I am a living reaction to my hurt,
a beginner cowboy trying to lasso
my traumas into the stable.
I am hardly ever stable.
Last week I busted my knuckle
on the steering wheel
because I believed for a moment
I'd made a wrong turn
when I became who I am.
I'd go into detail but it will hurt too much.
I hurt too much to be a saint.
Most of us do. My therapist
wants me to join a boxing gym
so to not break my skeleton
on what gets me to where I need to go,
so to not break that unspoken promise we all make
to be in real life whoever we are on instagram.

On instagram I am a cartwheel on the beach,
a typewriter collection, a pink umbrella
beneath a stormless sky, a snow angel
on my grandmother's grave.
On instagram I breathe
and a dandelion seed learns to fly.
On instagram I am never a weed,
never what kills the garden, never cold
as the frost, never punching the steering wheel
and icing my knuckles in a gas station parking lot.

But please, don't let me be
the kind of person whose crimes get revealed
after I die. May it all be written while I'm still alive,
even this: In the sixth grade, I left a note in a locker
that I still worry made a girl rethink her beauty
for the rest of her life.

NIGHT BLOOM
Crystal Williams

—For Jade, after Hayden

It makes no sense to say things will get better
because you will not understand until they are better
& they may not get better soon. There is always pain
in the world & you have seen so much of it.
I do not know how to explain other than to say,
I am so sorry your mother has died, Girl,
that her mother has turned her back, that your father
is a rogue & you are having to do this grown-up work alone.
I would like to tell you to be patient
but understand that right now you might only know fear.
Listen, then. & know this: it is okay to be fearful.
If you cannot believe that things will soften,
trust that I believe for you.
You will not remember all of this pain.
But when Darkness insists you attend his party
you will know the trapdoors & gloomy corners of that house.
& you alone will be able to find the garden
where beautiful Cereus is opening her eyes in the pitch black.

I WILL PRACTICE SELF-TALK

M. J. Fievre

When depression brings
a chill that settles inside me,
a marrow-deep tremor,
when the impulse of fear
burns my palms, I'll tell
myself stories
about the village of my youth,
where days were sunny and mild,
the skies a cheerful,
eggshell blue,
where the river shivered
bright rubble, & sisters
lured each other out
into the sunshine.
I'll describe out loud
the two-hour hike up a steep,
rocky mountain trail among the happy
fuchsia of bougainvillea;
the acacias that crossed their limbs
along the roads; the walls of jasmine,
their dark branches covered with
white corollas; the lady-of-night vines
opening their blue bells in the evening.
I will tell myself
that those sisters
climbed a mountain with their strong legs,
and that one pair of those legs
are mine.

8 belonging

What does it mean to feel a sense of belonging? The word itself is so close to *longing* that it contains that thirst for connection. Many of us grow up feeling separate from our peers and our families. My bitterest teen memories are of watching other kids laughing, standing on the outskirts of their easy fun.

The poets here acknowledge both the light and the shadow. They insist that connection is still possible. "Let's change the story," writes July Westhale, affirming that even after trauma, there can be love.

These poems remind me that we are still growing, discovering our own sacredness. "We know ourselves to be part of mystery," says Muscogee (Creek) poet Joy Harjo. In "Survival Guide," Joy Ladin explores the freedom of being "unfinished." This process of becoming ourselves takes years, decades, lifetimes. We must be patient.

I love how poetry creates moments of transformation. Mary Oliver offers a respite from shame and perfectionism. She follows the movements of the sun and the rain, promising, "You do not have to be good."

You are already enough, these poets say. You belong. You belong to our beautiful, broken, bewildering, wondrous world.

WILD GEESE

Mary Oliver

You do not have to be good.
You do not have to walk on your knees
for a hundred miles through the desert, repenting.
You only have to let the soft animal of your body
   love what it loves.
Tell me about despair, yours, and I will tell you mine.
Meanwhile the world goes on.
Meanwhile the sun and the clear pebbles of the rain
are moving across the landscapes,
over the prairies and the deep trees,
the mountains and the rivers.
Meanwhile the wild geese, high in the clean blue air,
are heading home again.
Whoever you are, no matter how lonely,
the world offers itself to your imagination,
calls to you like the wild geese, harsh and exciting—
over and over announcing your place
in the family of things.

THE RIDER
Naomi Shihab Nye

A boy told me
if he roller-skated fast enough
his loneliness couldn't catch up to him,

the best reason I ever heard
for trying to be a champion.

What I wonder tonight
pedaling hard down King William Street
is if it translates to bicycles.

A victory! To leave your loneliness
panting behind you on some street corner
while you float free into a cloud of sudden azaleas,
pink petals that have never felt loneliness,
no matter how slowly they fell.

SURVIVAL GUIDE

Joy Ladin

No matter how old you are,
it helps to be young
when you're coming to life,

to be unfinished, a mysterious statement,
a journey from star to star.
So break out a box of Crayolas

and draw your family
looking uncomfortably away
from the you you've exchanged

for the mannequin
they named. You should
help clean up, but you're so busy being afraid

to love or not
you're missing the fun of clothing yourself
in the embarrassment of life.

Frost your lids with midnight;
lid your heart with frost;
rub them all over, the hormones that regulate

the production of love
from karmic garbage dumps.
Turn yourself into

the real you
you can only discover
by being other.

Voila! You're free.
Learn to love the awkward silence
you are going to be.

DANCING WITH MY MOTHER AT A COUSIN'S BAT MITZVAH

Maya Stein

It's her hands that surprise me first,
the way they reach out at the song's first bars,
an eager schoolgirl's decisive clutch that brings my fingers
    into a C-curl.

Then we're off, in brilliant, twinned velocity
as Aretha launches into the meat of "Respect,"
and it's almost otherworldly how everything about us
comes into the sort of unison one never expects
after that languorous, bygone time in vitro.

But it does. Even twirling, Mom's got me in her hands,
as if I'd never left at all.

FOR MY DAUGHTER ON A BAD DAY

Kate Baer

Life will rough you up. Throw you to the
shore like a wave crashing—sand in your
hair, blood in your teeth. When grief sits
with you, hand dipped with rage, let it
linger. Hold its pulse in your hands. There
is no remedy for a bad haircut or ruined
love like *time*. Even when death is coming,
even when the filth rises in the back of
your throat—

this is not the worst of it. And if it is?
Listen for the catbird calling. No matter
the wreckage, they still sing for you.

LOVE ARRIVED MAY FIND US SOMEPLACE ELSE

July Westhale

The news did not shock the town,
used to being shocked, as one who wants
is used to being turned away.

Still, it was a good deal
to take in, though I was not the one
pregnant, and my sister
was sure in her resolve to keep it.

That summer I was determined to fall from a very tall bridge or sink under
a heavy lake, string pills with spread for a necklace, and eat them
while dancing. I was no longer able to deal with having been raped. During
which my sister grew thick, with a strange tadpole swimming in our
shared river.

I wanted
and she wanted
and he wanted, though he knew nothing
of want, not yet born
and we knew nothing of boys,
much less men.

Let's change the story, rewrite the foreshadow, strengthen the characters,
    forego the ending. It is with exclamations he is sentenced to the
world. On the way from the hospital, I gave him the commas of my fingers,
    to slow him. Without pause, he pulled them to his mouth, resolved to
keep them.

I want, but I know nothing—
understand nothing. Love
arrived may find us someplace else:
either born, or sleeping,
and what choice have we
but to rise, and outstretch,
say we planned for this,
and how good of you, to come at last.

FLOWERS #3

Joshua Jennifer Espinoza

Bring me to where it finally rains.

It is beautiful when the sun
goes down alone.

Above a river I say things
that no one hears.

It is summer forever in my heart and I am thirsty.

Push your fingers against me.
Separate the solid into liquid
and liquid into gas.

The way bodies are rendered on screens
makes me laugh at them.

My flesh on display absolves itself.
All of the pain it takes floats off into the sky.

Heaven is real for one moment at death.
One moment expands
and engulfs all other moments.

My love works the same way.

It is always dying and growing
at the same time.

Learning to love myself takes forever
and it never ends.

FOR KEEPS

Joy Harjo

Sun makes the day new.
Tiny green plants emerge from earth.
Birds are singing the sky into place.
There is nowhere else I want to be but here.
I lean into the rhythm of your heart to see where it will
    take us.
We gallop into a warm, southern wind.
I link my legs to yours and we ride together,
Toward the ancient encampment of our relatives.
Where have you been? they ask.
And what has taken you so long?
That night after eating, singing, and dancing
We lay together under the stars.
We know ourselves to be part of mystery.
It is unspeakable.
It is everlasting.
It is for keeps.

the poets

ARIA ABER is the author of *Hard Damage*, winner of the Prairie Schooner Book Prize in Poetry. Her work has appeared in the *New Yorker*, *Poetry*, the *Kenyon Review*, the *New Republic*, and elsewhere. She is the poetry editor of *BOAAT Journal* and holds fellowships from Kundiman, the Wisconsin Institute of Creative Writing, and New York University. ariaaber.com

ELIZABETH ACEVEDO is a *New York Times* bestselling author. She is the winner of a National Book Award, the Carnegie Medal, and the Michael L. Printz Award. Her books include *The Poet X* (HarperCollins 2018), *With the Fire on High* (HarperCollins 2019), and *Clap When You Land* (HarperCollins 2020). Acevedo is a National Poetry Slam champion and resides in Washington, DC, with her love. acevedowrites.com

KIM ADDONIZIO is the author of a dozen books of poetry and prose, including *Bukowski in a Sundress: Confessions from a Writing Life* and *Mortal Trash: Poems*. She has two books on writing poetry: *The Poet's Companion* (with Dorianne Laux) and *Ordinary Genius*. Her latest collection, *Now We're Getting Somewhere*, is due out from W. W. Norton in 2021. kimaddonizio.com

LESLIE MARIE AGUILAR originally hails from the heartland of Texas. She received her master of fine arts degree from Indiana University, where she served as the poetry editor of the *Indiana Review*. Her poems have appeared in

Callaloo, Hobart, Ninth Letter, Rattle, and *Sonora Review,* among others. She is the author of *Mesquite Manual* (New Delta Review 2015). lesliemarieaguilar.com

ANGÉLICA MARÍA AGUILERA is an internationally touring Chicana poet from the San Fernando Valley in Los Angeles. She was a finalist of the Women of the World Poetry Slam 2018 and the National Poetry Slam 2017. She is residing in Mexico City and working on her first book, *America as She.*

MAYA ANGELOU was a celebrated poet, memoirist, dramatist, actor, producer, filmmaker, and civil rights activist. Among her dozens of books are *I Know Why the Caged Bird Sings* and *Just Give Me a Cool Drink of Water 'Fore I Diiie.* Angelou received the National Medal of Arts in 2000, and was awarded the Presidential Medal of Freedom by President Barack Obama in 2010.

MARGARET ATWOOD is Canada's preeminent novelist and poet. She is the author of more than fifty books, which have been translated into over thirty languages. In addition to her beloved novels, she writes short stories, essays, screenplays, radio scripts, and children's books. She has received numerous awards, including the Booker Prize and the PEN Center Lifetime Achievement Award. Her dystopian novel *The Handmaid's Tale* has become an award-winning television series.

CAMERON AWKWARD-RICH is a poet, critic, and assistant professor of Women, Gender, Sexuality Studies at University of Massachusetts Amherst. He is the author of *Dispatch* (Persea Books) and *Sympathetic Little Monster*

(Ricochet Editions), a finalist for a Lambda Literary Award. He is working on a book about maladjustment in trans literature and theory. cawkwardrich.com

KATE BAER is a writer and poet based on the East Coast. Her work has been featured on Joanna Goddard's A Cup of Jo and in the *Huffington Post*. Her first book, *What Kind of Woman*, is available from Harper Perennial. katebaer.com

BLYTHE BAIRD is a spoken-word poet, educator, actor, and author of *If My Body Could Speak*. She has been featured in *Glamour*, the *Huffington Post*, *Everyday Feminism*, and more. In 2017, she won the ADCAN short film award, and in 2018, she graduated from Hamline University. Blythe lives in Minneapolis and is working on her next book. blythebaird.com

S. ERIN BATISTE is the author of *Glory to All Fleeting Things*. She is a Bread Loaf—Rona Jaffe Scholar in Poetry and a Cave Canem Fellow, and has received fellowships from Callaloo, SPACE on Ryder Farm, and Brooklyn Poets. Her Pushcart-nominated poems are anthologized and appear in *wildness*, *Paper Darts*, and *Puerto del Sol*, among other journals. batistewrites.com

TAMIKO BEYER is the author of *Last Days* (Alice James Books 2021) and *We Come Elemental* (Alice James Books 2013). Her poetry and prose have been widely published and awarded, including by PEN America. A social justice communications writer and strategist, Tamiko spends her days writing truth to power. tamikobeyer.com

SHEILA BLACK is the author of four poetry collections, including *Iron, Ardent*. She is a co-editor of *Beauty is a Verb: The New Poetry of Disability*. Her poems have appeared in *Poetry*, the *Birmingham Review*, *The Spectacle*, the *New York Times*, and more. She divides her time between San Antonio, Texas, and Washington, DC, where she works at AWP (Association of Writers & Writing Programs).

PAIGE BUFFINGTON is Navajo, of the Bear Enemies clan born for White People. She holds both bachelor of fine arts and master of fine arts degrees in creative writing from the Institute of American Indian Arts. Her work has appeared in *Terrain*, *Literary Hub*, and *Narrative*, among others. She teaches first grade outside Gallup, New Mexico.

HOLLY BURDORFF earned a master of fine arts degree in creative writing from the University of Alabama, where she was an editor of *Black Warrior Review*. Her work has appeared in *Shenandoah*, *The Common*, *Cimarron Review*, and elsewhere. She lives and works near Cleveland, Ohio. hollyburdorff.com

STEPHANIE BURT is a professor of English at Harvard. Her books of poetry and literary criticism include, most recently, *After Callimachus* (Princeton UP 2020), *Don't Read Poetry: A Book About How to Read Poems* (Basic 2019), and *Advice from the Lights* (Graywolf 2017), a National Endowment for the Arts Big Read selection. She has been fifteen for an improbably long time. Follow her on Twitter @accommodatingly.

MARCI CALABRETTA CANCIO-BELLO is the author of *Hour of the Ox* (University of Pittsburgh 2016), winner of the AWP Donald Hall Prize. She has received poetry fellowships from Kundiman, the Knight Foundation, and the American Literary Translators Association, among others. Her work has appeared in the *New York Times*, *Best Small Fictions*, *Best New Poets*, and more. marcicalabretta.com

KAYLEB RAE CANDRILLI is a 2019 Whiting Award Winner in Poetry and the author of *Water I Won't Touch* (Copper Canyon Press 2021), *All the Gay Saints* (Saturnalia 2020), and *What Runs Over* (YesYes Books 2017). Their work is published or forthcoming in *Poetry*, *American Poetry Review*, *Boston Review*, and many others. krcandrilli.com

LEILA CHATTI is a Tunisian American poet and author of *Deluge* (Copper Canyon Press 2020) and the chapbooks *Ebb* and *Tunsiya/Amrikiya*. She is the inaugural Anisfield-Wolf Fellow in Publishing and Writing at Cleveland State University, and her work appears in *Ploughshares*, *Tin House*, *American Poetry Review*, and elsewhere. leilachatti.com

FRANNY CHOI is the author of two collections of poetry, *Soft Science* (Alice James Books 2019) and *Floating, Brilliant, Gone* (Write Bloody Publishing 2014). She is a graduate of the Helen Zell Writers' Program at the University of Michigan, a Kundiman Fellow, and a member of the Dark Noise Collective. She lives in Northampton, Massachusetts. frannychoi.com

DOMINIQUE CHRISTINA is an award-winning poet, author, educator, and activist. She holds five national poetry slam titles, and her fourth book, *Anarcha Speaks*, won the 2017 National Poetry Series award. Her work is greatly influenced by her family's legacy in the civil rights movement and by the idea that words make worlds. Dominique is also a writer and actor for the HBO series *High Maintenance*. dominiquechristina.com

LUCILLE CLIFTON was a celebrated poet and children's book author. Her thirteen collections of poetry are known for their spare, punctuation-free style and their focus on African American experience and family life. A National Book Award winner and a Chancellor of the Academy of American Poets, Clifton was also the mother of six children.

NATALIE DIAZ is a Mojave poet and an enrolled member of the Gila River Indian Tribe. Her books include *When My Brother Was an Aztec* (Copper Canyon 2014) and *Postcolonial Love Poem* (Graywolf 2020). She is a MacArthur Foundation Fellow, a Lannan Literary Fellow, and a Native Arts Council Foundation Artist Fellow. Diaz teaches in the Arizona State University Creative Writing MFA program. nataliegermainediaz.com

AMY DRYANSKY's second book, *Grass Whistle* (Salmon Poetry 2013) received the Massachusetts Book Award for poetry. Her first, *How I Got Lost So Close to Home*, won the New England/New York Award from Alice James. She has two (almost) grown children and directs the Culture, Brain & Development Program at Hampshire College. amydryansky.com

DENISE DUHAMEL's most recent book of poetry is *Scald* (University of Pittsburgh 2017). Her other titles include *Blowout*; *Ka-Ching!* ; *Two and Two*; *Queen for a Day: Selected and New Poems*; *The Star-Spangled Banner*; and *Kinky*. Denise is a Distinguished University Professor in the master of fine arts program at Florida International University in Miami.

SAFIA ELHILLO is the author of *The January Children* (University of Nebraska Press 2017), *Girls That Never Die* (One World/Random House 2021), and a forthcoming novel in verse (Make Me a World/Random House 2021). Co-editor of the anthology *Halal If You Hear Me* (Haymarket 2019), she is a Wallace Stegner Fellow at Stanford University. safia-mafia.com

JOSHUA JENNIFER ESPINOZA is a trans woman poet living in California. Her work has been featured in *Poetry*, *Denver Quarterly*, *American Poetry Review*, *BuzzFeed*, *Poem-a-Day*, *Lambda Literary*, *The Offing*, and elsewhere. She is the author of *There Should Be Flowers* (Civil Coping Mechanisms 2016). joshuajenniferespinoza.com

TARFIA FAIZULLAH is the author of *Registers of Illuminated Villages* (Graywolf 2018) and *Seam* (SIU 2014). Her writing has appeared in *BuzzFeed*, *PBS News Hour*, the *Huffington Post*, *Poetry*, *Ms.*, and elsewhere. The recipient of a Fulbright fellowship and three Pushcart prizes, Tarfia was recognized by Harvard Law School in 2016 as one of 50 Women Inspiring Change. Born in Brooklyn, New York, to Bangladeshi immigrants and raised in Texas, she lives in Chicago. tfaizullah.com

M. J. FIEVRE is a writer, editor, educator, translator, and entrepreneur. Born in Port-au-Prince, Haiti, M. J. began her publishing career as a teenager and has authored nine books in French. She is the author of *Happy, Okay? Poems about Anxiety, Depression, Hope, and Survival* and *Badass Black Girl: Questions, Quotes, and Affirmations for Teens.* She helps others write their way through trauma, build community, and create social change. mjfievre.com

ANDREA GIBSON (they/them/theirs) is a queer poet and author who has been touring internationally for two decades. The first winner of the Women's World Poetry Slam, Gibson has released seven albums and authored four collections of poems. Their work riots against gun violence, homophobia, and white supremacy, while jubilating gender expression, queer love, and the will to stay alive. Gibson's most recent book, *Lord of the Butterflies*, was selected as the Independent Publisher Poetry Book of the Year. andreagibson.org

NIKITA GILL is a British Indian writer and the bestselling author of six volumes of poetry. Her books include *Wild Embers: Poems of Rebellion, Fire, and Beauty* and *Great Goddesses: Life Lessons from Myths and Monsters* (Penguin 2019). Follow her on Instagram @nikita_gill.

AMANDA GORMAN is the Inaugural Youth Poet Laureate of the United States. In 2020, she graduated cum laude from Harvard with a degree in Sociology. She has written for the *New York Times* The Edit newsletter and has two books forthcoming with Penguin Random House. amandascgorman.com

WENDY GUERRA was brought up in Cienfuegos, Cuba, and resided in Havana, where she persisted as an almost unknown poet and novelist, now of international importance. Her work has been translated into thirteen languages and published in the *New York Times*. Some of her books are *Everyone Leaves*, *A Cage Within*, and *Revolution Sunday*.

JOY HARJO is an internationally renowned performer, writer, musician, and activist. She is a member of the Muscogee (Creek) Nation and the twenty-third Poet Laureate of the United States. A Chancellor of the Academy of American Poets, Joy has authored nine books of poetry, several plays and children's books, and a memoir, *Crazy Brave*. Her latest poetry collection is *An American Sunrise*. joyharjo.com

RAGE HEZEKIAH is a New England–based poet and educator whose poems have been anthologized, co-translated, and published internationally. She has received fellowships from Cave Canem, MacDowell, and the Ragdale Foundation. Rage is the author of *Unslakable* (Paper Nautilus Press 2019) and *Stray Harbor* (Finishing Line Press 2019). ragehezekiah.com

JP HOWARD is an educator, literary activist, curator, and community builder. Her debut poetry collection, *SAY/ MIRROR*, was a Lambda Literary finalist. She co-edited *Sinister Wisdom Journal 107: Black Lesbians—We Are the Revolution!* JP has received fellowships from Cave Canem, VONA, and Lambda and curates Women Writers in Bloom Poetry Salon. jp-howard.com

MARIE HOWE is an award-winning poet and educator. She is the author of four poetry collections, most recently *Magdalene*, and a Chancellor of the Academy of American Poets. The former Poet Laureate of New York State, Howe teaches at New York University and Sarah Lawrence College. She lives in New York City with her daughter. mariehowe.com

LAURA KASISCHKE has published nine collections of poetry, most recently *Where Now: New & Selected Poems* (Copper Canyon 2018). Her collection *Space in Chains* won the National Book Critics Circle Award. A critically acclaimed novelist as well as a poet, Kasischke has published numerous novels and a book of short fiction. She teaches in the master of fine arts program at the University of Michigan.

SARAH KAY is a New Yorker, a poet and educator, and the founder and co-director of Project VOICE. She is the bestselling author of four books of poetry and a celebrated performer in more than twenty-five countries. An alum of Brown University, Kay received an Honorary Doctorate of Humane Letters from Grinnell. Follow her on Twitter @kaysarahsera.

JANE KENYON was a beloved poet and the author of five books during her lifetime, including translations of the Russian poet Anna Akhmatova. She grew up in the Midwest and settled on a New Hampshire farm with her husband, the poet Donald Hall. The former Poet Laureate of New Hampshire, Kenyon died of leukemia at the age of forty-seven.

JOY LADIN has published nine books of poetry, including *The Future is Trying to Tell Us Something: New and Selected Poems*, and two Lambda Literary Award finalists, *Impersonation* and *Transmigration*. Her second collection, *The Book of Anna*, was reissued in 2020. Links to her work are available at wordpress.joyladin.com.

DORIANNE LAUX is the author of six collections of poetry, most recently *Only As the Day Is Long: New & Selected Poems* (W. W. Norton 2019). She is a Chancellor of the Academy of American Poets and the coauthor (with Kim Addonizio) of *The Poet's Companion: A Guide to the Pleasures of Writing Poetry*. Laux lives in North Carolina and teaches in the master of fine arts program at North Carolina State University. doriannelaux.net

MELODY LEE has published four poetry collections, including *Moon Gypsy*, *Vine*, *Season of the Sorceress*, and *Lilies & Lace & Dark Pretty Things*. Her poems have been featured live on Shrimp Shack Ipswich Community Radio, A Better Media Today, Creative Talents Unleashed, and Her Red Pen. Follow her on Instagram @melodyleepoetry.

ADA LIMÓN is the author of five books of poetry, including *The Carrying*, which won the National Book Critics Circle Award for Poetry. Her fourth book, *Bright Dead Things*, was a finalist for the National Book Award. Limón teaches in the Queens University of Charlotte master of fine arts program and works as a freelance writer in Kentucky. adalimon.com

LYNN MELNICK is the author of the poetry collections *Refusenik, Landscape with Sex and Violence*, and *If I Should Say I Have Hope. I've Had to Think Up a Way to Survive*, a book about Dolly Parton that is also a bit of a memoir, will be published next from University of Texas Press. lynnmelnick.com

MARY MERIAM co-founded Headmistress Press and edits the *Lavender Review: Lesbian Poetry and Art*. She is the author of the collections *My Girl's Green Jacket* (2018) and *The Lillian Trilogy* (2015), both from Headmistress Press. Meriam's poems appear in many journals, most recently *Poetry, Prelude*, and *Subtropics*. marymeriam .blogspot.com

NAOMI SHIHAB NYE is an award-winning poet and author. Born to a Palestinian father and an American mother, she has published more than thirty volumes, including poetry, children's books, young adult fiction, essays, and novels. Nye has received numerous honors for her work, including the Award for Lifetime Achievement from the National Book Critics Circle. She is currently the Poetry Foundation's Young People's Poet Laureate and lives in San Antonio, Texas.

SHARON OLDS has been writing candid, boundary-pushing poems about the body since 1980. The author of a dozen collections of poetry, most recently *Arias* (Knopf 2019), she captures the experience of sexuality, motherhood, desire, and grief. Olds's work has received many honors, including the Pulitzer Prize. She is a former Chancellor of the Academy of American Poets and lives in New York City.

MARY OLIVER was a beloved, bestselling American poet whose poems celebrate the natural world. The winner of the National Book Award and the Pulitzer Prize, Oliver was a prolific author of both poetry and prose, and published more than thirty volumes in her lifetime. She lived for more than forty years in Provincetown, Massachusetts, with her partner, the photographer Molly Malone Cook.

SARA PETERS was born in Antigonish, Nova Scotia, and lives in Toronto. She completed an MFA at Boston University and was a Stegner Fellow at Stanford University. Her work has appeared in *Slate*, the *Threepenny Review*, and *Poetry* magazine, among many other literary journals. Her first book was *1996* (House of Anansi Press 2013).

ALISON PRINE's debut collection of poems, *Steel* (Cider Press Review 2016) was named a finalist for the 2017 Vermont Book Award. Her poems have appeared in *Ploughshares*, the *Virginia Quarterly Review*, *Five Points*, *Harvard Review*, and *Prairie Schooner*, among others. She lives and works in Burlington, Vermont. alisonprine.com

FARIHA RÓISÍN is an Australian Canadian multidisciplinary artist known largely for her work as a writer, editor, and podcaster. She is the author of two poetry collections, *How to Cure a Ghost* and *Being in Your Body*, and the novel *Like a Bird*. Her work explores wellness, Muslim identity, race, self-care, pop culture, and film. Follow her on Instagram @fariha_roisin.

ALISON C. ROLLINS's poems have appeared in *American Poetry Review*, the *New York Times Magazine*, *Poetry*, and elsewhere. She is a recipient of the Poetry Foundation's

Ruth Lilly Fellowship and a National Endowment for the Arts fellowship. She works as a lead teaching and learning librarian at Colorado College. Her debut poetry collection is *Library of Small Catastrophes* (Copper Canyon Press 2019). alisoncrollins.com

SAHAR ROMANI's poems appear in *Poetry Society of America*, the *Adroit Journal*, *The Offing*, the Asian American Writers' Workshop's *Margins*, and elsewhere. Trained as a geographer, Sahar completed a PhD from Oxford. She received her master of fine arts degree in poetry from New York University, where she teaches expository writing. Born and raised in Seattle, she lives in Queens, New York.

NATALIE SCENTERS-ZAPICO is a poet, educator, and activist from the sister cities of El Paso, Texas, USA, and Ciudad Juárez, Chihuahua, México. She is the author of two poetry collections, most recently *Lima :: Limón* (Copper Canyon Press 2019), and has received many awards and fellowships for her work. She is a professor at the University of Puget Sound. nataliescenterszapico.net

BRENDA SHAUGHNESSY is the author of five poetry collections, including *The Octopus Museum* (Knopf 2019), a *New York Times* Notable Book. Recipient of a 2018 Literature Award from the American Academy of Arts and Letters and a 2013 Guggenheim Foundation Fellowship, she is professor of English at Rutgers University–Newark. brendashaughnessy.com

EVIE SHOCKLEY is the author of four books, most recently *semiautomatic* (Wesleyan 2017), which won the Hurston/Wright Legacy Award in Poetry. Her other books include *the new black* (Wesleyan 2012), also a Hurston/Wright Award winner, and *Renegade Poetics: Black Aesthetics and Formal Innovation in African American Poetry* (University of Iowa Press 2011). Shockley is professor of English at Rutgers University—New Brunswick.

ELIZABETH SPIRES is the critically acclaimed author of seven collections of poetry, including *Worldling, The Wave-Maker,* and *A Memory of the Future.* She has also written seven books for young readers, including *The Mouse of Amherst,* a celebrated picture book that offers children a first taste of Emily Dickinson's poetry. She lives in Baltimore, Maryland, and teaches at Goucher College.

MAYA STEIN is a Ninja poet, writing guide, and creative adventuress. Since June 2005, she has kept a weekly short-form poetry practice called 10-Line Tuesday. When she's not searching for metaphors, she can be found wandering the backroads by tandem bicycle, reviving her left-hand hook shot, and online at mayastein.com.

MELISSA STEIN is the author of the poetry collections *Terrible blooms* (Copper Canyon Press 2018) and *Rough Honey,* winner of the APR/Honickman First Book Prize. She has received awards and fellowships from the National Endowment for the Arts, Pushcart, Bread Loaf, MacDowell, and Yaddo. She is a freelance editor in San Francisco. melissastein.com

BIANCA STONE is a poet and visual artist. Her poems have appeared in the *New Yorker*, *Poetry*, and *Green Mountains Review*. She is director of programs at the Ruth Stone Foundation in Goshen, Vermont, and the author of *Someone Else's Wedding Vows* and *The Möbius Strip Club of Grief* (Tin House Books 2018).

TALIN TAHAJIAN grew up near Boston. She reviews, occasionally, for the *Kenyon Review Online*. Her poetry has appeared in *Poetry*, *Narrative Magazine*, *Best New Poets*, and elsewhere. She edits poetry for the *Adroit Journal*, and is a Zell Postgraduate Fellow of the Helen Zell Writers' Program at the University of Michigan. talintahajian.com

MICHELLE TEA is the author of more than a dozen works for adults and children, including several memoirs, a poetry collection, and a young adult fantasy trilogy about mermaids. She is the founder of RADAR Productions, a literary nonprofit that supports queer-centric projects, and the creator of Drag Queen Story Hour in San Francisco. Follow her on Twitter @TeaMichelle.

CLARA BUSH VADALA is a North Texas poet and veterinarian. Her poems have appeared in *SWWIM*, *Thimble*, and *Lammergeier* and been featured at Texas Tech's Sowell Conference and the Houston Poetry Festival. She has two poetry collections: *Prairie Smoke* and *Beast Invites Me In*, both available from Finishing Line Press.

JULY WESTHALE is an essayist, translator, and the award-winning author of five collections of poetry, including *Trailer Trash* and *Via Negativa*. Her most recent work can be found in *McSweeney's*, *Prairie Schooner*, and the *Huffington Post*, among others. She's also the co-founder of *PULP* Magazine, a multimedia sex, sexuality, and reproductive rights publication. julywesthale.com

DIANA WHITNEY writes across the genres with a focus on feminism, motherhood, and sexuality. Her first book, *Wanting It*, became an indie bestseller in poetry. Her personal essays have appeared in the *New York Times*, *Glamour*, the *Washington Post*, and many more. A feminist activist in her Vermont hometown and beyond, Diana works as an editor and a yoga teacher. diana-whitney.com

RACHEL WILEY is a queer, biracial poet and performer from Columbus, Ohio. She is a faculty member at the Pink Door Writing Retreat for women and nonbinary writers of color. Rachel has performed at slam venues, colleges, and festivals nationwide. Her first book, *Fat Girl Finishing School*, was rereleased by Button Poetry in 2020. Her second, *Nothing Is Okay*, received the Ohioana People's Choice Award.

CRYSTAL WILLIAMS is a poet and essayist, and the author of four collections of poetry, most recently *Detroit as Barn*. She is associate provost for diversity and inclusion and professor of English at Boston University. Crystal works to help make ours a more loving and just world—both in her creative writing and as a senior leader in higher education. crystalannwilliams.com

the illustrators

CRISTINA GONZÁLEZ is a graphic designer and illustrator based in Quito, Ecuador, who creates bold and colorful art images, richly textured and often with a retro look. Her work talks about sexuality, mental health, self-love, and equity, supporting all gender expressions and diversity of races and body shapes, with the desire to empower women of all ages to feel comfortable and confident with exactly who they are. snakesandroses.com

KATE MOCKFORD is an illustrator living in Cornwall, United Kingdom. Her illustrations are sensitive, colorful, and playful, with a splash of texture and striking compositions. Through visual storytelling, Kate has a special talent of illustrating life into being. She is represented by Lipstick of London. Follow her on Instagram @katemockford.

STEPHANIE SINGLETON is a freelance illustrator with a love for all things decorative and surreal. She is currently based in Toronto, Canada. You can see more of her work at stephaniesingleton.com.

PERMISSIONS/ CREDIT LINES

Joy Ladin, "Survival Guide." From *The Future is Trying to Tell Us Something: New & Selected Poems*, published by Sheep Meadow Press, copyright © 2017. Reprinted with permission of the author.

Dorianne Laux, "Fast Gas" from *What We Carry*. Copyright © 1994 by Dorianne Laux. Reprinted with the permission of The Permissions Company, LLC on behalf of BOA Editions, Ltd., boaeditions.org.

Melody Lee, "Growing Up." From *Season of the Sorceress: Poetry and Prose*. Copyright © 2019 by Melody Lee. Reprinted with permission of the author.

Ada Limón, "How to Triumph Like a Girl." From *Bright Dead Things* by Ada Limón (Minneapolis: Milkweed Editions, 2015). Copyright © 2015 by Ada Limón. Reprinted with permission from Milkweed Editions. milkweed.org

Lynn Melnick, "Landscape with Clinic and Oracle." From *Landscape with Sex and Violence*, published by YesYes Books. Copyright © 2017 by Lynn Melnick. Reprinted with permission.

Mary Meriam, "The Mockers." From *My Girl's Green Jacket*, published by Headmistress Press. Copyright © 2018 by Mary Meriam. Reprinted with permission of the author.

Naomi Shihab Nye, "The Rider" from *Fuel*. Copyright © 1998 by Naomi Shihab Nye. Reprinted with the permission of The Permissions Company, LLC on behalf of BOA Editions, Ltd., boaeditions.org.

Sharon Olds, "I Go Back to May 1937." From *The Gold Cell* by Sharon Olds, copyright © 1987 by Sharon Olds. Used by permission of Alfred A. Knopf, an imprint of the Knopf Doubleday Publishing Group, a division of Penguin Random House LLC. All rights reserved.

Mary Oliver, "Wild Geese." From *Dream Work*, copyright © 1986 by Mary Oliver. Used by permission of Grove/Atlantic, Inc. Any third party use of this material, outside of this publication, is prohibited.

Sara Peters, "Rehearsal." From *1996*, copyright © 2013 by Sara Peters. Reprinted with permission from House of Anansi Press, Toronto. houseofanansi.com

Alison Prine, "Rearview Mirror: February." From *Steel*, published by Cider Press Review. Copyright © 2016 by Alison Prine. Reprinted with permission of the author.

ACKNOWLEDGMENTS

My heartfelt thanks goes out to the poets and artists whose phenomenal work made this book possible.

I also wish to thank my wonderful editor, Mary Ellen O'Neill, whose passion for poetry catalyzed this project. Thanks to designer Rae Ann Spitzenberger, and the whole team at Workman, for bringing *You Don't Have to Be Everything* to life.

I'm grateful to my brilliant agent, Lisa DiMona, and her assistant, Lauren Carsley, both of whom sustained me with their faith and enthusiasm. Additional thanks to James Crews and Lynn Melnick, for wisdom and reassurance—and to all the writers in my Tuesday night salon and Montague poetry workshop, for creative solidarity and inspiration.

Thanks to students at Brattleboro Union High School, the Putney School, and Vermont Academy for reading and responding to some of these poems.

My deepest gratitude to my family—Tim, Ava, and Carmen Whitney. Your love and support keep me grounded and lift me up, every day.